CURRENTS OF

MEDIAEVAL THOUGHT

With special reference to Germany

By MICHAEL SEIDLMAYER

Translated by
D. BARKER

OXFORD
BASIL BLACKWELL
1960

Authorised translation of 'Weltbild und Kultur Deutschlands
im Mittelalter' Band I, Abschnitt 6, by permission of
Akademische Verlagsgesellschaft Athenaion

STUDIES IN MEDIAEVAL HISTORY

Edited by GEOFFREY BARRACLOUGH

Vol. V

CURRENTS OF MEDIAEVAL THOUGHT WITH SPECIAL REFERENCE TO GERMANY

First printed in this translation
© BASIL BLACKWELL, 1960

PRINTED IN GREAT BRITAIN
BY A. T. BROOME AND SON, 18 ST. CLEMENT'S, OXFORD
AND BOUND BY THE KEMP HALL BINDERY, OXFORD

CONTENTS

GENERAL BIBLIOGRAPHY AND ABBREVIATIONS

The bibliography has been restricted to a selection of essential items, preference being given to important monographs and recent works containing further helpful references.

For specialist literature the appropriate articles in the following works of reference are recommended:

LThK=*Lexikon für Theologie und Kirche* (2nd edn., 1930–38).
RGG=*Die Religion in Geschichte und Gegenwart* (2nd edn., 1927–32).
Dict. d'hist.=*Dictionnaire d'histoire et de géographie ecclésiastique* (1912–).
Dict. Theol.=*Dictionnaire de Théologie catholique*, ed. A. Vacant and E. Mangenot (1902–).

JOURNALS:

AK=*Archiv für Kulturgeschichte* (1903–).
DA=*Deutsches Archiv für Erforschung des Mittelalters* (1937–).
GRM=*Germanisch-Romanische Monatsschrift* (1909–).
HJb=*Historisches Jahrbuch der Görresgesellschaft* (1880–).
JbLit=*Jahrbuch für Liturgiewissenschaft* (1921–). Now *Archiv für Liturgiewissenschaft*, 1950–.
Sav=*Zeitschrift der Savignystiftung für Rechtsgeschichte* (1880–).
St. Ben=*Studien und Mitteilungen aus dem Benediktinerorden* (1880–).
VLit=*Deutsche Vierteljahresschrift für Literaturwissenschaft und Geistesgeschichte* (1923–).
ZAlt=*Zeitschrift für deutsches Altertum und deutsche Literatur* (1841–).
ZPh=*Zeitschrift für deutsche Philologie* (1869–).
Revue d'histoire ecclésiastique (Louvain, 1900–) contains extensive bibliography.
Speculum. A Journal of Medieval Studies (Cambridge, Mass., 1926–).
Traditio. Studies in Ancient and Medieval History, Thought and Religion (New York, 1943–).

SOURCES:

Monumenta Germaniae Historica.
Migne, *Patrologia latina.*
S. Gaselee, *The Oxford Book of Medieval Latin Verse* (Oxford, 1928).
Series of medieval German literary works: *Altdeutsche Textbibliothek* (ed. G. Baesecke, 41 vols., Heidelberg, 1882–); *Deutsche Texte des Mittelalters* (Preussische Akademie der Wissenschaften, 43 vols., Berlin, 1904–).
K. Müllenhof, W. Scherer, *Denkmäler deutscher Poesie und Prosa aus dem 8.-12. Jahrhundert* (3rd edn., Berlin, 1892).

GENERAL WORKS:

The Cambridge Mediaeval History (8 vols., 1911–1936).

G. Steinhausen, *Geschichte der deutschen Kultur* (2 vols., 3rd edn., Leipzig, 1929).

G. Grupp, *Kulturgeschichte des Mittelalters* (6 vols., Paderborn, 1921–25) —immense amount of material.

R. W. Collins, *A History of Medieval Civilization in Europe* (Boston, 1936).

K. Vossler, *Medieval Culture*, transl. W. C. Lawton (2 vols.).

F. B. Artz, *The Mind of the Middle Ages* (New York, 1953).

The following volumes of the *Handbuch der Kulturgeschichte* (ed. H. Kindermann):

P. Kletler, *Deutsche Kultur zwischen Völkerwanderung und Kreuzzügen* (Potsdam, 1934).

H. Naumann, *Deutsche Kultur im Zeitalter des Rittertums* (Potsdam, 1938).

H. Gumbel, *Deutsche Kultur von der Mystik bis zur Gegenreformation* (Potsdam, 1936).

Chr. Dawson, *The Making of Europe* (reprint, London, 1948).

Chr. Dawson, *Medieval Essays* (London/New York, 1953).

M. Seidlmayer, *Das Mittelalter. Umrisse und Ergebnisse des Zeitalters* (Regensburg, 1948).

CHURCH HISTORY:

A. Hauck, *Kirchengeschichte Deutschlands* (5 vols., some reprinted, Leipzig, 1922–29)—also a standard work on cultural history.

A. Fliche and V. Martin, *Histoire de l'église depuis les origines jusqu'a nos jours* (9 vols., Paris, 1934–44)—down to 1198.

G. Schnürer, *Kirche und Kultur im Mittelalter* (3 vols., Paderborn, 1924–29).

H. Feine, *Kirchliche Rechtsgeschichte*, Vol. I (Weimar, 1950).

H. Günter, *Psychologie der Legende. Studien zu einer wissenschaftlichen Heiligengeschichte* (Frankfurt, 1949).

K. D. Schmidt, *Die Bekehrung der Germanen zum Christentum* (Göttingen, 1935–)—appearing in instalments; the most thorough work on the subject.

J. Herwegen, *Antike, Christentum und Germanentum* (Salzburg, 1932).

Fr. v. Bezold, *Das Fortleben der antiken Götter im mittelalterlichen Humanismus* (Bonn, 1922)—stimulating study.

LITERATURE:

M. Manitius, *Geschichte der lateinischen Literatur des Mittelalters* (3 vols., Munich, 1911–1931)—to the end of the twelfth century.

J. de Ghellinck, *La littérature latine au moyen âge* (2 vols., Paris, 1939).

F. J. E. Raby, *A History of Christian Latin Poetry from the Beginning to the Close of the Middle Ages* (2nd edn., Oxford, 1953).

F. J. E. Raby, *A History of Secular Latin Poetry in the Middle Ages* (2 vols., Oxford, 1934).

G. Ehrismann, *Geschichte der deutschen Literatur bis zum Ausgang des Mittelalters* (4 parts, Munich, 1918–1934).

W. Stammler, *Die deutsche Literatur des Mittelalters* (4 vols., Berlin/Leipzig, 1933–1953).

H. Schneider, *Heldendichtung, Geistlichendichtung, Ritterdichtung* (2nd edn., Heidelberg, 1943).

J. Schwietering, *Die deutsche Dichtung des Mittelalters*—in the ' Handbuch der Literaturwissenschaft '—(Potsdam, n.d.).
(For the history of thought in the Middle Ages the last two are most valuable.)

E. Norden, *Die antike Kunstprosa vom 6. Jahrhundert vor Christ bis in die Zeit der Renaissance* (2 vols., Leipzig, 1898).

E. R. Curtius, *Europäische Literatur und lateinisches Mittelalter* (2nd edn., Berne, 1954)—essays which contain a great deal of material and reveal many problems.

PHILOSOPHY AND THEOLOGY:

B. Geyer, *Die patristische und scholastische Philosophie* (11th edn., Berlin, 1927–; reprinted Tübingen, 1951).

M. de Wulf, *Histoire de la philosophie mediévale* (3 vols., 6th edn., 1934–47).

E. Gilson, *La Philosophie au Moyen Âge* (2nd edn., Paris, 1944).

M. Grabmann, *Geschichte der scholastischen Methode* (2 vols., Frankfurt, 1909–11).

M. Grabmann, *Mittelalterliches Geistesleben. Abhandlungen zur Geschichte der Scholastik und Mystik* (2 vols., Munich, 1936).

R. Seeberg, *Lehrbuch der Dogmengeschichte*, Vol. III. (4th edn., Leipzig, 1930).

ECONOMIC AND SOCIAL HISTORY:

R. Kötzschke, *Allgemeine Wirtschaftsgeschichte des Mittelalters* (Jena, 1924).

J. Kulischer, *Allegemeine Wirtschaftsgeschichte des Mittelalters und der Neuzeit, Vol. I* (Munich/Berlin, 1928).

The Cambridge Economic History of Europe (Vol. I, 2nd edn., 1942; Vol. II, 1952).

J. W. Thompson, *An Economic and Social History of the Middle Ages, 300–1300* (2nd edn., New York/London, 1951).

H. Pirenne, *Economic and Social History of Medieval Europe* (Eng. transl., 1936).

C. Delisle Burns, *The First Europe* (London, 1947).

A. v. Martin, *Kultursoziologie des Mittelalters*—in ' Handwörterbuch der Soziologie,' ed. A. Vierkandt—(Stuttgart, 1931).

W. Schwer, *Stand und Ständeordnung im Weltbild des Mittelalters*, (2nd edn., Paderborn, 1952)—brief but particularly penetrating study.

E. Tröltsch, *Die Soziallehren der christlichen Kirchen und Gruppen* (Tübingen, 1912).

ART:

G. Dehio, *Geschichte der deutschen Kunst*, Vols. I–III, with appropriate volumes of plates (Berlin, 1922–27).

H. Weigert, *Geschichte der europäischen Kunst* (Stuttgart, 1951).

J. Sauer, *Symbolik des Kirchengebäudes und seiner Ausstattung in der Auffassung des Mittelalters* (2nd edn., Freiburg, 1924).

K. Künstle, *Ikonographie der christlichen Kunst* (2 vols., Freiburg, 1926–28).

CHAPTER I

FROM LATE ANTIQUITY TO CHARLES THE GREAT
FOUNDATIONS AND SYNOPSIS OF THE PERIOD

THESE studies in the history of thought and civilization are concerned in the first instance with the *German* sphere which formed the nucleus of the mediaeval Empire. And yet, if they are really to fulfil their intended purpose, they must of necessity take in the whole of Europe. For, in the Middle Ages, it is no more possible to speak of a ' German culture ' as a segregated, independent unit than it is to speak of an Italian, a French or an English culture. Rather they are all to be considered as elements and branches of a common European society, each representing a special form or extension of a single, comprehensive culture, the culture of the West. Individually they are dovetailed parts of the European structure and they exist and develop only as such. Only by placing them in the perspective of Western European culture as a whole can we obtain a true pattern of German thought and life in the Middle Ages—or of that of any other of the great nations. It is against this wider background that we shall best gain insight into the peculiar features of each and their individual qualities, objectives and achievements, and so be able to assess both their strength and their weakness.

The main reason, however, which makes it necessary to ignore geographical boundaries and to look back to periods when neither the word nor the concept 'German' was in existence, is that in the Middle Ages German thought and German civilization were shaped by pre-existing, non-German elements. Civilization was still international in spirit. We can be almost certain that no culture has ever been formed by the independent efforts of the people it represents. To some degree foreign cultural influences are always operative in the process. A new civilization emerges only when foreign contributions have been assimilated and fused into a fresh basis. But in the case of the northern peoples, whose rise to power ushered in the period we call ' The

Middle Ages ', and from whom a specifically German people began to take shape in the ninth and tenth centuries, the situation is still more complicated. In their efforts to reach a higher level of existence it was their peculiar task to have to assimilate a civilization the whole development of which had taken place in a foreign scene and whose form and content had been fashioned without the slightest contribution from themselves. They were probably the first peoples to have to do this, and civilization was handed on to them as a ' finished article ' imported from a world which, however decadent and moribund, was still infinitely superior to their own.

The first problem facing these new peoples was the task of assimilating a completely foreign way of life, which they had to take over in all its aspects and to learn as best they could. They had to learn very much as the schoolboy learns his lessons, and their schooldays lasted for centuries. It is, of course, true that we remain ourselves even while learning; and so, from the very beginning, and to a far greater extent than we are aware, much of our own nature and personality creeps into the process. This is an important factor which will demand further attention (see below, p. 28 sq.). Nevertheless, the fact remains that the higher culture which the Germanic peoples so ardently desired remained for centuries a foreign body in the Germanic world. Its foreign and external nature was emphasized by being expressed in Latin, a foreign language, which meant that it remained exclusive and confined to a comparatively small circle of ' educated ' men. Gradually this stage of purely assimilatory learning was left behind and the peoples of northern Europe began to reveal their own powers. In time they were able to judge the value of this foreign inheritance, sometimes criticizing it quite bitterly. Finally they grew out of the primary stage of second-hand knowledge and built a world of higher intellectual and spiritual values according to their *own* laws.

The Middle Ages in western Europe were born of the meeting between the Hellenistic civilization of the Roman Empire and the Germanic peoples of northern Europe. The one was old and world-weary, the other youthful and vital. The Roman world of the Mediterranean basin was slowly sinking into a grave of its own making. It was as though it had savoured and exhausted all that life had to offer and arrived at its natural end. In Pope Gregory the Great's words, it was a world ' bowed down with age and hurrying with increasing suffering towards its death '. On the other hand, in the north, groups of 'primitive' peoples were forcing their way to the fore. These peoples, although they had a thousand years of history behind them, were only just beginning to knock on the portals which give access to ' culture '. They were ' barbarians ' in so far as they had an unbounded confidence in their own strength but were still unaware of their own gifts and potentialities. The contrast is clear at every point. On the one side we have a slow decline from healthy vitality to an uneasy doubting of the value of all earthly enterprise and the material gains which it might bring. It is a decline into silent, despairing resignation in the face of the needs and sufferings of this world; it is a decline into timid introspection, taking refuge in an inner world which could not be attacked. In a few individuals, it is true, the dying embers of Roman valour flared up anew, only to succumb in the end to the unswerving progress of events. In northern Europe, on the other hand, we see peoples overflowing with vitality, who grasp greedily and with childish credulity at the tempting possessions of a newly discovered, higher civilization. As yet they are without any clear objective, they lack self-discipline or firm purpose and are still incapable of directing their own feet along the paths which could lead them to higher accomplishments.

Thus the torch of culture slips from the hands which have so long held it aloft and falls to hands which are not yet capable of lifting it up again by their own unaided efforts. It was under such auspices that the culture of the Middle Ages was born. It was meanly and scantily endowed and its early character was to be decisive for long ages to come. Throughout the old Roman world there now begins a shrinkage and regression of the whole scope of life; economic and political organization, personal feelings and thought in general are all affected. Social life contracted and concentrated on the defence of the basic things. It was reduced to its bare essence, rejecting luxury and non-essentials, just as a tree in winter withdraws its life-giving sap in order to ensure its bare existence. It could not maintain the form and content of a higher, more delicate and varied conduct of life. This process of contraction entered its decisive stages as a result of the terrible catastrophes which afflicted the western core of the ancient world in the second half of the sixth century. The Gothic wars and the Lombard conquests marked the turning point. North of the Alps the lowest ebb was reached in the middle of the eighth century and the tide did not turn until political and cultural life were consolidated afresh under the Carolingians.

At this point a significant contradiction, rooted in Christianity, becomes evident. It is in the nature of Christianity that it stimulates at the same time the will to withdraw from the world and the will to be active in the affairs of this world; and this dualism decides from this time onwards the course of mediaeval culture. Rarely, perhaps never, have these two attitudes to life been so closely inter-connected as in this seething age of ferment which laid one world in its grave and gave birth to another. The one was the attitude of Christian otherworldliness. At that time in particular it was understood in the extreme, ascetic sense of ' turning one's heart completely from this world '. Many, like Gregory the Great, regarded this as the purpose and justification of their whole life. And yet it was precisely the visible and tangible embodiment of this transcendentalism, the church, which became the repository of all remaining external activities, shaping both the social and private life of the age. The struggle for worldly wealth had been exposed as futile by bitter striving for the simplest necessities of life; but now it was given a new and vigorous impulse by being yoked to the church's doctrine of salvation. It was given purpose and justification and it became again worth pursuing with vigour and energy. Cultural life, both material and spiritual, found refuge in the precincts of the church —almost the only place where there was still physical and moral protection for it. But only those aspects which were capable of being linked closely with the other-worldly objective, only those aspects which served the church's specific policy of furthering religion in this world, were allowed. Everything else—the refinements of external civilization, science and knowledge for their own sake, the independent values of aesthetics, the richness of a full and sensitive spiritual life in the individual—all this was excluded and, for lack of independence and intrinsic value, finally atrophied and died. From now on, the nature and degree of all earthly values were judged according to the demands of the *conscious* preparation for the life beyond; there was no power to question the scale of values of religious transcendentalism.

It is well known that by the time this great process of cultural shrinkage and regression came to a close at the end of the period of migrations, material culture and techniques for the most part and intellectual activity completely and exclusively lay in the hands of the church. But this was only the external expression of a more fundamental change, by which the whole approach to life on this earth was made religious and subordinated to the specific tenets and demands of monks. Life was divested of its worldly values to an extent unique in the history of Christendom.

During the turmoil which finally gave a new face to the western world the inheritance was being amassed which later antiquity was to pass on to the Middle Ages. This legacy was to help the new age to furnish its own intellectual life for many centuries—almost half the mediaeval epoch—after which it implemented it and rounded it off in its own fashion. It is, therefore, essential to review more closely the determinative features of this age of transition and to get to know the teachers who set the standards of the Middle Ages.

THE TEACHERS OF THE EARLY MIDDLE AGES

The pre-Christian, pagan element in this inheritance was derived, as is well known, not from the civilization of the Greek and Roman city-states but from the Hellenism of the late Roman Empire. In the course of time this Hellenism itself had changed. Its line of development had carried it in the direction of Christianity. It was this alone which made possible the thorough mingling of Hellenistic philosophy and early Christian theology and, over a much larger field, the complete assimilation of one world by another. The pagan intellectual leaders of the first centuries of the Christian era had moved towards a system which was, in Dilthey's phrase, 'metaphysical and monotheistic'. Philosophy had been transformed into a religious and transcendental approach to life. All thought revolved round the concepts of ' ultimate reality ' and ' greatest good,' and these were represented by something above and beyond all earthly phenomena, as something absolute and divine. The whole universe, man included, was permeated by forces radiating from the ' ultimate reality '. Mortal man was able to perceive the whole cosmic order by immersing himself in it speculatively and mystically. He could raise himself to the sphere of the absolute by leading a morally impeccable life. In this way the theories of Neoplatonism and of Roman Stoicism were brought into close alliance.

By thus placing man's ' genuine ' values beyond the natural needs of his body an entirely spiritual approach to life was achieved. The cosmos as a whole may be permeated with divine order and beauty, nevertheless, the tangible ' nature ' and assets of this world and, above all, the physical side of humanity had to be stripped of all real value. Compared to the ' eternal verities ' they were only mirages, pale creatures of the moment. Only by using his inner freedom to rise above them, to transcend, or shut them out of his life, would man attain real happiness and his purpose in life. At the very least, man was not interested in the natural, physical world. This elimination of all worldly attributes is seen in the ethereal quality, transcending all sensuousness, of the Byzantine style in art, in the new philosophical speculation and ethical values, and in the trend in the natural sciences away from material things to symbolism, mysticism and magic. Every sphere of life was affected. The convulsed world, in which the threat of destruction was the constant fear of large numbers of people, in which the fight for life was so ugly and brutal, no longer seemed to be worth any whole-hearted effort. It was inevitable that the world should repel precisely the more sensitive minds and direct them to the ' inner life '.

The other-worldly abjuration of this life and the stern moral ideals of the late classical world were all that Christianity could wish for. And yet, the two worlds are divided by a chasm which was all the more effective because it was concealed. The ancient world argued that man's rational mind should achieve its own salvation by lifting itself up into the spheres of ' true being ' and ' greatest good '. The Middle Ages sought religious salvation for man broken under his burden of sin through the external agency of that mercy procured by the divine suffering on the cross. It was no accident that Augustine's final penetration to true Christian faith came as a result of a negative assessment of classical civilization. In spite of all this the frontiers of these two worlds blur and fade away again and again. Throughout the Middle Ages, right down to the age of Humanism, these two worlds, which were basically so unlike and opposed to one another, were mingled and confused. Contemporaries seem to have regarded them like two brothers, differing only in minor features.[1]

The most significant example of this is provided by the finest monument of free, philosophic piety, the *Consolatio Philosophiae* of Boethius, a book which, as no other, commanded the warm veneration of the Middle Ages. Boethius was a Christian, author of an essay on the Trinity, and, at the time of writing the *Consolatio*, in prison and facing death. Even a hundred years after Augustine he still sought and found his ' consolation ' not in the message of sin, mercy and salvation of Christian belief, but in the elevation of a reflective mind above the material world. This is his way to the ' greatest good ' to which he was led by a blend of Neoplatonism and Stoicism. His carefully polished language turns the work into an aesthetic jewel. Thus he deprives many earthly attributes and values of all justification, often by means of acrobatics of reasoning no less involved than those we find in later mediaeval treatises preaching contempt for the world. Yet his book remains an impressive witness to the extraordinary vitality of this pre-Christian philosophy, even in its last days. The Middle Ages, however, treated this book as the supreme expression of their own conception of a truly Christian renunciation of all worldly things. It became part of the basic equipment of every

[1] For the above, cf. M. Rostovtzeff, *The Social and Economic History of the Roman Empire* (2 vols., 1926; 2nd edn., 1956); H. J. Marrou, *St. Augustin et la fin de la culture antique* (Paris, 1938), together with the supplementary volume: *Retractatio* (Paris, 1949); E. Fleury, *Hellénisme et christianisme, St. Grégoire et son temps* (Paris, 1931); J. Bidez, *La vie de l'empéreur Julien* (Paris, 1930); Fr. Kaphan, *Zwischen Antike und Mittelalter. Das Donaualpenland zur Zeit Sankt Severins* (Munich, n.d.); Fr. Klingner, *Römische Geisteswelt* (Sammlung Dieterich, Leipzig, 1943); B. Schweitzer, *Die spätantiken Grundlagen der mittelalterlichen Kunst* (Leipzig, 1949); and P. E. Hübinger, ' Spätantike und frühes Mittelalter. Ein Problem historischer Periodenbildung ', VLit XXVI (1952), 1 sqq., with a useful bibliography.

cloister and cathedral school. Alfred the Great ordered it to be translated into Anglo-Saxon as early as the ninth century; Notker the German of St. Gall (d. 1022) translated it into German for his pupils—*propter caritatem discipulorum*; from the thirteenth century onwards it was translated repeatedly into German and there were countless commentaries on its form, language and content. Scarcely a single work of ancient classical literature, and not even many of the Church Fathers, claimed such universal esteem as this ' Consolation of Philosophy ' in the Christian Middle Ages.

Through Boethius the spirit of the ancient world had spoken its last independent word. All that comes after him belonged to a world in which clerical values were determinative, in which worldly accomplishments were allowed only so much scope as was necessary for them to fulfil their functions as auxiliaries to the Christian striving towards the life hereafter. This scope was naturally subject to widely divergent interpretations.

Boethius' contemporary, Flavius Aurelius Cassiodorus, who survived him by more than half a century (d. *circa* 583), produced a programmatic introduction to the new period. He, also, delighted in scholarship and the refined pleasure it brings, but for him pure intellect was not the mainspring; for him the Christian faith had become the genuine inner substance. In the second half of his life, having withdrawn from the futile political scene, he was wholly concerned to save the treasures of the ancient world for succeeding generations before it was too late. To this end he gathered a community of monks around him on his estate at Vivarium in southern Italy. Scholarship and culture realized that their safest refuge was in the cloister. There Cassiodorus drew up the programme of culture which he presented in his ' Primer of Divine and Worldly Knowledge ' (*Institutiones divinarum et saecularium litterarum*). In two respects it provided the watchword of the times to come. In the first place it set forth the ' ideal of learning of mediaeval Christian traditionalism ' (H. Loewe); that is to say, it renounced individual, creative work and limited itself to conserving and handing on the classical inheritance. Cassiodorus himself faithfully observed this in his numerous other writings. Secondly, it demanded the compression of all profane instruction into the framework of the *septem artes liberales* (see below, p. 13 sqq.). These would have to be mastered first so that the divine sciences—the Bible, the Church Fathers, the historians of the church—could be understood. The strict subordination of profane intellect to religious purposes was thus firmly established.

Cassiodorus' aim was still a double one: *salus animae et saecularis eruditio*. But the current of life which accepted only the one religious objective had already started to swell and was to continue in full spate throughout the Middle Ages. Benedict of Nursia (d. *circa* 547), ' the father of Western monasticism ', was not exactly opposed to either theological or profane studies; rather, he was indifferent to them and they played no part in his rules of monastic life. Several other factors, however, lend an extraordinary and perhaps unique historical importance to his work.

First of all, the Benedictine Rule which he drew up was truly Roman in its order, taste and wise restraint. It aimed at subjugating human passions—including radical, self-destroying asceticism—and at organizing them in a balanced, communal way of life. The basic idea was the formation of a *militia Christi* in which the principle of isolation from the world was to render productive service to the world in return. For it demanded of the monk regular manual work as a way to salvation and thereby firmly established the ethical dignity of work—a value which was equally foreign both to classical antiquity and to the pagan Germanic world. And so, although it cannot have been foreseen by Benedict, there arose out of the economic structure which he prescribed for his cloister —' a closed, self-sufficing community of producers and consumers '—the system which was to become the supreme model of the age of natural economy. There was no other system efficient enough to offer serious competition.

The Rule also contained a precept of tremendous importance for the education of the peoples of northern Europe. Previously they had known only those social dispositions which are derived directly from primitive nature and tradition: family, clan and tribal community. Benedict's Rule gave them the first example of a way of life which can be attained only by self-discipline and the observance of the rules and principles of a planned social life. It was, of course, a programme of religious asceticism; both north and south of the Alps the period was incapable of understanding any other kind of programme. Through this teaching they gradually learned that human society need not always be governed by primitive instincts but that it can and must be subjected to rational control, and that only a healthy competition between mind and nature can foster a higher culture worthy of the name. It was a teaching which bore fruit far beyond the confines of monastic life.

These features made the Benedictine Order so much superior to other orders that it virtually banished them all from the scene after the end of the eighth century, and, if we include its Cistercian branch, remained unchallenged in its superiority until the thirteenth century. As is well known, by far the greatest credit for clearing and cultivating new land in western Europe especially in Germany, in these centuries when the main settlements took place, falls to Benedictine monks. And after intellectual work had been admitted to the Benedictine cloister, the Order also became the foremost repository of all cultural and artistic pursuits. The first steps in this direction had been prompted quite early by the work of Cassiodorus and a few other monastic groups—particularly the Celtic Irish monks (see below, p. 35). The exact contribution of the Benedictines to the development of Western culture eludes precise assessment, but its significance for the western world and northern Europe in particular is immeasurable. Erich Caspar was not exaggerating when he called Benedict's *Regula* ' one of the most fateful documents of all time '.[1]

Pope Gregory the Great (590–604) was the first to make a deliberate attempt to destroy the philosophic ideals of the ancient world. Although we may be charmed by the genuine, human warmth of his personality we cannot but be surprised at the contempt with which in his writings he rejects all intellectual and aesthetic culture—at least in theory. For him this is not only useless, but even dangerous, ballast to the true Christian. In the theological field he replaced deeper penetration into the

[1] E. Caspar, *Geschichte des Papsttums* ii (Tübingen, 1933), 321.

essence of Christian faith with completely naive and often ridiculously far-fetched, moralizing allegories based on Holy Writ. He encouraged an insatiable belief in miracles and relics which, in effect, banished all intellectual judgement. Things are worthy of consideration only in so far as they appear to be directly applicable to the purpose of moral teaching or spiritual deliverance from this world. But Gregory showed by his own example that this may be paired with a resolute struggle against worldly cares and trials. He must have been fully aware of the intellectual retrogression which his teaching signified when he said that Augustine offered ' fine wheat ' in comparison with his own contribution of 'husks'. As Manitius says, with Gregory ' the link between classical philosophy and Christian speculation is broken '.[1] But for centuries to come it was only in the debased form served up by Gregory that the primitive mind of the northern peoples was able to digest theological nourishment. The expression ' Simplism ' which has been coined for this programme of *scienter nescius et sapienter indoctus* (Gregory on Benedict), is justified in spite of all arguments to the contrary.

Nevertheless, behind this Simplism a new vitality was developing. It was a vitality which was still ' barbarous ' enough but all the same powerful and heavy with a great future. For now there was a definite objective which overruled all others. Herein lies the vital contrast between the new period and the late classical period with its wearied, sceptical resignation, its intellectualism and aestheticism.

Gregory's comprehensive works became the chief source of authority of the Middle Ages, and his rulings were observed even when they were detrimental to the purposes and interests of later generations. There was, admittedly, an immediate need for simplifying spiritual concepts; and much of Gregory's work is of a high quality. His *Regula Pastoralis* in particular, is a work of considerable value, showing fine psychology and human tolerance as well as giving much genuine spiritual guidance. But against this are to be balanced the ponderous extravagances and deformities of clerical intellectualism as applied to

---

[1] M. Manitius, *Geschichte der lateinischen Literatur des Mittelalters* i (Munich, 1911), 64.

religion, such as the excessive passion for allegory, miracles and relics, which obsessed the Middle Ages and made intellectual enlightenment impossible. For this, also, Gregory, as the revered model of the whole period, invested with almost unimpeachable authority, must be held largely responsible.

Even so, Gregory's simplistic ' vulgar catholicism ' never achieved absolute predominance. After him the two main bastions of classical culture during the period of the migrations, Spain and Britain, each produced a man whose genuine search for knowledge led him into the same paths as Cassiodorus. The importance of Isidore of Seville and the Venerable Bede as teachers of the Middle Ages must be rated very high.

Isidore of Seville (d. 636, as archbishop), one of the greatest encyclopaedists of all time, assembled in his *Etymologiae* (i.e. descriptive explanations of words) every imaginable item of knowledge which the ancient world, heathen or Christian, could offer. He started with theology and proceeded via history, geography, natural science, folk-lore, etc., right down to the functional attributes of daily life, such as the tools of the craftsman and the implements of the peasant. Down to the thirteenth century it was the supreme reference book of the Middle Ages—an encyclopaedia in the modern sense of the word.

In England the Venerable Bede (d. 735), who had been brought up as a monk from his earliest childhood, produced a mosaic of works in exegesis of the Old and New Testaments —metrics, orthography, mathematics, nature-lore, history, and chronology. It was due to him that it became the general custom to count the years from the birth of Christ. The scope and range of the polymath of the early Middle Ages are typified in Bede. Towards the end of his life he made the following confession: 'And while I have observed the regular discipline and sung the choir offices daily in church, my chief delight has always been in study, teaching and writing '. This is a simple, restrained expression of the noblest aspect of the new mediaeval mentality.[1]

---

[1] For the above, cf. Boethius, *Consolatio Philosophiae*, transl. H. F. Stewart and E. K. Rand (1918). E. K. Rand, *Founders of the Middle Ages* (1928); M. L. W. Laistner, *Thought and Letters in Western Europe*, A.D. 500–900 (London 1931); H. R. Patch, *The Tradition of Boethius, A Study of his Importance in Mediaeval Culture* (New York, 1935); H. Löwe, ' Cassiodor ', *Romanische Forschungen* LX (1948), 320 sqq.;

THE SEVEN LIBERAL ARTS

All the knowledge and wealth of civilization which these two most important teachers of the new epoch transmitted over the watershed between the ancient and the mediaeval worlds was pressed into the pattern of the ' Seven Liberal Arts '. Alcuin called them the ' Seven Pillars of Wisdom ' and they did in fact dominate all education for more than five hundred years with a tenacity which was quite extraordinary even in the conservative Middle Ages. A brief examination of this system will serve to round off this sketch of the general state of education in the first half of the Middle Ages.

The seven subjects were divided into two groups, ' Trivium ' and ' Quadrivium '. The ' Trivium ' consisted of Grammar, Dialectic and Rhetoric. *Grammar*, called the ' Queen of Sciences ', was mainly concerned with the simple rules of grammar and spelling. It is significant that even the most eminent scholars of the time busied themselves with expositions of such elementary subjects! The teaching of idioms and of figures of speech such as metaphors was also part of grammar. In this subject several books of instruction were available, dating mainly from the fourth to the sixth centuries, such as Donatus, Martianus Capella and Priscian. In the more ambitious schools grammar included the reading of the classical authors—sometimes more than a dozen of them were offered. Virgil was always the first favourite. On the whole these authors were used merely to provide practical examples of the rules of grammar, and in time this led more and more to the use of scanty extracts (*exempla*) in schools. This was countered again as early as the twelfth century, particularly in

A. van de Vijver, ' Cassiodore et son oeuvre ', *Speculum VI* (1931), 244 sqq.; E. Brehaut, *An Encyclopedist of the Dark Ages, Isidor of Seville* (New York, 1912); A. H. Thompson, *Bede, His Life, Time and Writings* (Oxford, 1935); W. Levison, *England and the Continent in the Eighth Century* (reprint, 1949); J. Herwegen, *Der heilige Benedikt* (1926); The general historical importance of Benedict is extremely well treated in E. Caspar, *Geschichte des Papsttums* ii, (Tübingen, 1933), 320 sqq.; cf. also Paul Lehmann, ' The Benedictine Order and the Transmission of the Literature of Ancient Rome in the Middle Ages ', *Downside Review*, 1953, 407 sqq.; J. Herwegen, *Sinn und Geist der Benediktinerregel* (Einsiedeln/Cologne, 1944); E. C. Butler, *Benedictine Monachism* (2nd edn., 1924); Ph. Schmitz, *Histoire de l'ordre de St. Bénoit* (6 vols. [Vol. I 2nd edn., 1948], Maredsous, 1942–49); P. Battifoll, *S. Grégoire le Grand* (2nd edn., Paris, 1928). The best characterization of Gregory is to be found in E. Caspar, *op. cit.* ii, 306, sqq.

the Anglo-Norman region of north-west Europe, by a humanistic reaction which insisted on the whole book being read so that it could be appreciated as a work of art.

Dialectic taught the logical sequence of argument and abstract, conceptual thinking. For the Germanic peoples, whose thought had previously been limited to concrete, pictorial premisses this change to abstract thinking was a radical transformation. Hence it is easy to understand why the Middle Ages had to ' go to school' for generation after generation. Indeed, dialectic constituted a very minor part of the curriculum down to the eleventh century. And when dialectic led to independent thinking and the subject began to claim a place in the front rank of studies it implied the coming of a new epoch.

Rhetoric was, in the words of Hrabanus Maurus, ' a wider, more explicit exposition of that which dialectic teaches with concise brevity '. As rhetoric was primarily a product of the more lively and mobile southern temperament it did not thrive particularly well among the ponderous Germans and there was nothing more than elementary stylistics (*ars dictaminis*) devoted to composing official letters and deeds.

So the Trivium, especially in its reduced form as taught in the more humble schools, provided only the groundwork of elementary education. The derivation of the word ' trivial' still reminds us of this. Following the Trivium the Quadrivium introduced the higher branches of knowledge: Astronomy, Arithmetic, Geometry, and Music.

Of these the most highly developed was *astronomy* which is one of the oldest lores of man in all civilizations. It was also of particular, practical importance as the necessary basis for calculating times and dates such as Easter.

Arithmetic was complicated by the use of the Roman system of numerals. Apart from its use in ready-reckoning it gave rise to endless possibilities of extravagant number-symbolism. All the single-figure numbers and many of the multi-figure numbers were invested with symbolic power, a ' higher meaning '. There were the Trinity, the four elements, the four periods of the world, the four rivers of Paradise, the seven churches and angels of the Apocalypse or, as the sum of three and four, signifying the union of the divine with the earthly—spirit and body. Ten was the 'complete number'. What they called *geometry* was in fact mostly geography. Hrabanus Maurus defined it as 'the science of the immovable universe' or 'the measurement of the earth'.

Music was closely connected with the numbers of arithmetic in theory, according to the old Pythagorean system. In practice its first objective as a school subject was to train pupils to sing the choral services in church.

Empirical experience, the visible and tangible world, is almost completely ignored in the Seven Arts; nor had classical antiquity ever paid much attention to this sphere of knowledge and education. Apart from astronomy almost all that was done in the way of natural science amounted to arbitrary and gaudy collections of curiosities from foreign countries and strange peoples. Much faith was placed in the healing powers of certain animals, plants and stones—particularly precious stones. These also, like the numbers, were the subjects of interminable arguments about their symbolic meaning (see below, p. 90 sq.)—yet another item in the inheritance from the late classical world.

There was one further point in support of the Seven Arts. Cassiodorus first mentioned it, and it was then taken up and extended, particularly by the Venerable Bede: namely, that the whole system is vouched for in the Holy Scriptures, 'just like the wine in the grape or the tree in the tiny seed'. For them the Bible represented not only the word of God but also the primer of basic knowledge with which God had endowed man. It must therefore be a work of literary art. Hence, the study of the Seven Arts was a necessary preparation for the pursuit of the true faith and, conversely, biblical texts must be the best *exempla* in the teaching of basic grammar and stylistics. Charles the Great, in a letter to the important monastery of Fulda, said: 'The better a reader has previously mastered the discipline of letters the quicker he will be able to understand the spiritual message of the Scriptures'. It would be difficult to find better evidence of the extent to which the worldly aims of education had been absorbed into the demands of religion and theology.

The general lines of development of Western culture for more than fifteen hundred years would be contained in a history of this system. It would bring out the shrinking and simplifying process by which classical antiquity changed into a new epoch as well as the process of renewal which set in at the peak of the Middle Ages. In the ancient (Greek) world the arts, which were not then limited to seven, were regarded as general education. They were the basis from which to progress to something higher, which could be reached only through the study of philosophy. But by the last phases of antiquity, philosophy no longer counted as an independent discipline; the Seven Arts were already regarded as the whole range of culture. The system was rounded off and established by Boethius, Cassiodorus, Isidore of Seville and others. The little that remained of philosophy—and even theology!—was portioned out more or less crudely among the various subjects of the Seven Arts. Apart from a few specifically mediaeval introductions, the system might be compared to the syllabus of a humanistic grammar school of the old type; what the 'Arts' did not cover was not worth teaching.

Towards the end of the twelfth century a new institution began to take the lead in education and scholarship. This was the University, which was called ' Studium generale '. Even here the ' Faculty of Arts ' formed the foundation on which all the other sciences had to build. Curtius considers that Thomas Aquinas ' ushered in a new era '[1] when he asserted that ' the Seven Liberal Arts do not make sufficient provision for theoretical philosophy ' —meaning that philosophy should be an independent subject. This is not to say that the arts had lost all importance by the late Middle Ages, or even by the period of Humanism; it only means that their power to limit the scope of intellectual endeavour had been broken. After a lapse of some eight hundred years learning in the true sense of the word was revived. Independent, inquiring minds were once more allowed to develop freely, as they had done in the ancient classical world.

The Unity of the Middle Ages

The intellectual foundations of the Middle Ages as outlined above were the basis of a civilization which was the common property of the whole of Christian Europe. This unity of culture

[1] E. R. Curtius, *European Literature and the Latin Middle Ages* (London, 1953), 57.

delimits the first half of the mediaeval period, and the gradual disintegration and final collapse of this unity is the theme of the second half. Unity in Christianity is the keynote of the whole period, first as the mainspring of European society and then as the source and target of the revolts against it in the second half of the period.[1]

Both corner-stones of mediaeval life and philosophy, unity and Christianity, stand in need of careful analysis. They have so often been devalued and distorted by hasty judgements and misused as the catchwords of romantic idealism.

In the first place the unity of this Christian civilization was encouraged by natural conditions. The Middle Ages as a new epoch in history developed in the territories of primitive, un-developed peoples at a time when they were still living close to nature, characterized by an essentially agrarian economy, which contrasted markedly with the more versatile, urban, monetary system still operating elsewhere in Europe. This agrarian economy made private initiative almost impossible, and was thus one of the main factors in the conservatism of the Middle Ages. Feudalism, a social order of farmer aristocrats, derives from this factor its principle of pre-determined birth-rank which completely ignored the merit of individual achievement. It was not a horizontal structure which permitted the equal coexistence of classes and individuals, but rather, a vertical, graduated hierarchy. But it did bind all men into a firmly fused, organic society.

A further cause of unity was the fact that the numerous small tribes or peoples in these territories were not greatly differentiated from one another by political or social institutions. They had no distinctive political institutions of their own. Nor did they think of themselves as differing one from another. There was nothing to interfere with the establishment of an *Imperium*, founded to a large extent on non-political, religious ideals; the northern world had no intellectual or spiritual assets which might, by their very presence, have opposed the order of universal

---

[1] C. Fr. Specht, *Geschichte des Unterrichtswesens in Deutschland bis zur Mitte des 13. Jahrhunderts* (Stuttgart, 1885); J. E. Sandys, *A History of Classical Scholarship* (3 vols., Cambridge, 3rd edn., 1920); For p. 13 sqq. cf. particularly E. R. Curtius, *European Literature and the Latin Middle Ages*, 36 sqq. and 446 sqq.

Christendom. The whole region was moved by the same patterns of thought, the same values, feelings and tempers and, therefore, was uniformly open to all cultural influences brought to bear upon it. Later it was moved, by a belief that it was being improved by these influences, to an intense effort to assimilate them. The same items of knowledge, purveyed by the same methods of teaching and the same ' school-books ', were accepted by everybody as being true and correct. Uniformity throughout Christian Europe was almost inevitable.

The few possibilities of deviation which remained were narrowly restricted. But in this context the terms ' type ' and ' norm ' mean something formed spontaneously, without conscious effort; there was no necessity to subject either peoples or individuals to a régime of uniformity and conformity by force of arms. The civilization with which we are concerned was shaped by the organic development of a common outlook resulting from its natural origins and descent as well as by intellectual tradition and authority. It had no need to overcome any individual characteristics or interests—not even such as might have been justified and constructive.

If this were a complete and precise assessment of the facts of the position arising from the unity of western Christendom, however, historical development from this point would appear impossible. But the full picture was quite different. Nicolas Cusanus, the most brilliant German thinker of the Middle Ages, said, ' In one contrast there always lies hidden the origin of the next contrast '—and so, ' the beginning of one thing is always the ending of another '. He thus recognized that there can be no static condition in the life of man, only dynamic progress and a succession of events—in fact, history.

Mediaeval uniformity had always been full of such latent conflicts. The most obvious lay in the duality of Empire and Papacy which ultimately led to the death-struggle of the epoch. The conflict started at the very beginning of the Empire on Christmas Day in the year 800. For the ' universality ' of the Empire was only an ideal; the unity which it implied was only approximately realized.

In the same way there were anomalies in the economic and

social structure, for some finance and trade had survived and there were occasional, limited opportunities to rise in social rank. The intellectual incompatibility of the primitive Germanic mentality and the imported foreign culture was stressed at the beginning of this chapter. We must also take into account the fact that there had always been some tension between the religious outlook imposed by monasticism and the inarticulate spiritual demands of secular life. In the educational system (i.e. the Seven Arts) tradition and authority shaped scholars' minds until they made themselves independent of this control and finally turned against its authority. But, for the time being, all these concealed tensions remained well below the surface. In each instance one of the opposing tendencies was overwhelmingly strong, so that it never came to a real contest, except in a few exceptional cases which only serve to confirm the rule. Nevertheless, it must be kept in mind that this common order of life, whose values, forms and aims were apparently equally valid for all peoples and individuals, was not free from cross-currents.

In dealing with any aspect of mediaeval civilization the fundamental point to remember is that the Middle Ages grew out of a ' primitive ', incipient phase of historical development —a situation unique in history. As this natural basis was left behind the period lost its early, external uniformity and developed a much more complicated interplay of all material and intellectual factors. It simply reached out beyond itself.

The natural motive forces of civilization—mind, will, temperament and courage—developed separately along their own lines, and sooner or later men became conscious of the potentialities of each of these and acquired new ambitions. The ' will to power ' had only to exceed slightly its normal, instinctive limits to produce a political ideology—i.e. a deliberately organized objective for its ambition, for which it was concerned to find a just, legitimate basis. Whether or not this ideology was morally justified was not important enough to deter men from making vigorous and insistent efforts to achieve their aims.

The classic example of this in the Middle Ages was the rise of France in the twelfth and thirteenth centuries. Classes, social factions and wealthy individuals became aware of their positions in and their claims on society; they were no longer satisfied with the narrow limits imposed upon them within the existing order. They all sought to assert their own peculiar right to live and their own natural claim to power, with the result not only that the uniform structure of mediaeval life as a whole was disrupted but that a bitter struggle for existence between these various forces was inevitable. The same symptoms can be seen in the individual. Every window through which he viewed the world —understanding, beauty, love, nature, social intercourse and material wealth—offered a sunlit prospect of a higher, richer and more refined form of life.

Even personal religious experience both demanded and promised more than the aloof, sacramental provisions of the church were able to fulfil either in fact or in theory. Just as the distinguishable groups and sections of this society, once its unity was broken, lost all bearings in this struggle, so also the individual mind and spirit were disturbed and could no longer establish equilibrium among their contradictory powers and desires. The dissolution of the universal order of things, which had comprised human existence *in toto*, imposed a price of endless confusion and pain. The whole of the later Middle Ages bears witness to this fact. The Middle Ages inherited features which proved to be uncontrollable once their inherent problems quickened into activity.

The Church in the Early Middle Ages

Christianity, however, remained the foundation and the agent which moulded and formed this western cultural unity. Superficially the concept ' Christian culture ' seems to give rise to no questions or problems at all; actually it could well contain more problems than are to be found at any other period in European history. For two distinct historical fields merge in it. To a certain extent they are complementary, but their origins and objectives are quite different and they flourish under totally different conditions. The church was faced with the problem of eliminating the inevitable frictions but was never more than moderately successful. As Guardini has said, the church was forced into an ' uncomfortable attitude '. Even in the two hundred years of late classical antiquity, during which Christianity alone was accepted as the state religion and thus had the power to influence all aspects of public and cultural life, it was scarcely aware of any specifically ' Christian ' culture and even less inclined to put anything of this nature into practice. Consciously or unconsciously it seemed to adopt the attitude 'My kingdom is not of this world', and all attempts at an indiscriminate ' Christianization ' of secular civilization, as well as all material representations of religion, were regarded with critical reserve. On the whole the church was content to suppress and eradicate as far as possible those elements of its heathen inheritance which were directly opposed to its beliefs and ethical standards. We have seen already in Boethius, how profane cultural values and Christian belief may exist side by side in the same individual and, although their position is perhaps not quite the same, some religious poets and preachers—Ennodius, Sidonius Apollinaris, Venantius Fortunatus—show a similar combination.

The intention to ' Christianize ' this world as it stands, to make ' Christian culture ' into a programme, was an innovation of the early Middle Ages. The plan was extraordinarily fertile but it also laid great burdens both on culture in general and on religion; the period shows ample evidence of both effects. But it was perhaps the most creative and productive undertaking of the whole period and one which was repeatedly revived during several centuries.

The essential points of the programme have been described above. All aspects of man's existence which mattered at all had to be placed in an other-worldly perspective. Otherwise they had no legitimate purpose or standing.

Two trends in this other-worldly scale of values have already been distinguished. One aim was to subordinate the natural disposition of mortal man to the service of the life hereafter, and so give it some ultimate justification; the other approach considered life on earth essentially inferior and detrimental to the supreme objective and therefore tried to reduce intellectual activity to a minimum, or even dispose of it entirely, wherever possible. The principle of both trends, then, was to make the things of this world, including the essential qualities of humanity, quite powerless by divesting them of all intrinsic worth. In both cases the aim was the realization of the Kingdom of God on *this* earth. Conversely, there was no place in the programme for even a relative autonomy of intellect and culture. They were simply not recognized as aspects of natural, human endeavour, which are completely neutral and indifferent to religion.

And yet, the Europe for which this programme was prescribed retained its natural ways of life which were entirely independent of Christianity, just as the classical world had done. Indeed, many of its motives were in direct contradiction to the teachings of the Gospels. Whereas in the ancient world the elements of paganism which could not be destroyed were modified and crudely adapted to Christianity, the mediaeval world made such anomalies more serious by finding positive justification for them. The church sanctioned them on religious grounds so that they could be incorporated on an equal footing into the Christian order of things. It is essential to realize that a ' Christian culture ' free of such contradictions was beyond the conception of both the early and the mature Middle Ages.

The whole *populus christianus* which purported to represent ' God's Kingdom on Earth ' was divided into sharply defined castes according to rank of birth—nobles, free and unfree. The vast majority of Christians were constrained into the ranks of serfs and villeins of all grades down to veritable slaves who could be bought and sold. They were condemned to a preordained dependence which involved a tremendous economic burden and inevitable social inferiority. The Christians of later antiquity never tried to abolish this social and legal system on the grounds that it was contrary to Christian teaching; in their view it was a matter to which the church should be indifferent (1 Cor. vii, 21) as long as it conformed to the minimum demands of Christian neighbourly love. Even St. Benedict obviously reckons with the existence of serfdom in the economic organization of his monastery; only the cloister itself, the inner domain dedicated to the *militia Christi*, was to ignore the earthly distinction between free and unfree. The mediaeval mind, however, refused to be satisfied with this compromise, for it could understand and accept the actual world only in so far as it conformed to its ideal world (see p. 28).

Everything had to conform to the ideal of Christian other-worldliness. And so, as W. Schwer says, ' with naive insouciance the church projected the existing social facts into the Bible and then, reversing the process, referred to the latter to justify the former '.[1] The most gifted woman of the epoch, Hildegard of Bingen (see below, p. 92 sq.), considered it intolerable that noble and common nuns should live together in the same house. If this were allowed ' the high moral standards of the cloister would be destroyed, for they (the nuns!) would tear one another to pieces in their hatred, if the higher classes should descend to the lower and the lower rise up to their superiors. . . . For God makes the same distinctions among His people on earth as He does in heaven, where He divides them up into angels, archangels, cherubim and seraphim—and all are beloved of God '. This goes further than admitting distinctions of rank and class into the monasteries. It establishes the fact that the divisions of society on earth, organized in Hildegard's view in ' a great many steps and degrees ', reflect the divine precept of the heavenly hierarchy. This is the decisive argument.

In mediaeval law it was a generally accepted fact that the aristocratic upper class had the right to resort to revenge or self-help in the form of feuds, in spite of attempts to curtail their more destructive excesses. Military law in war and corporal punishment in civilian life were as pitiless and cruel as those of any non-Christian community. In the ancient world Christianity had never disputed the necessity of waging war and bearing arms, regarding it rather as a necessary evil and a divine punishment. The idea of endowing war with religious justification and approval, however, was even more foreign to it. But war and battle were the very breath of life of the Germanic people—or, at least, of the relatively small proportion of noble leaders. So, even though it was a slow and difficult task to distort the teachings of the Gospel so radically (see Matt. xxvi, 52), in the long run it was inevitable that religious sanction should be given to bloody wars of annihilation in the name of the Cross of Christ, and to the

---

[1] W. Schwer, *Stand und Ständeordnung im Mittelalter* (Paderborn, 1952), 33.

use of armed might on behalf of oppressed Christians and
' widows and orphans '.[1] In the end men killed in battle against
the heathen were accorded the same halo as the suffering Christian
martyrs.

The ancient world had entrusted the Emperor with the
protection of the church, a function which gave him important
religious duties, extending even to decisions on dogma and
belief. The Middle Ages went beyond this combination of secular
and spiritual powers. Rulers were ordained and anointed with
holy oil just like bishops (the oil was sent directly down from
heaven for the Kings of France), and the duty of leading the
army in battle was specified as part of their religious duties. By
proclaiming the Emperor *Vicarius Christi, Imago Dei, typum
Salvatoris nostri gerens*, etc., the Christian Middle Ages abolished
all barriers between ' the worldly ' and ' the spiritual '. The
Emperor symbolized just as much as the Pope the highest degree
in the Church. The ' turning-point of Canossa ', as A. Mayer-
Pfannholz[2] called the first serious opposition to this sancti-
fication of the office of ruler, which came to a head in the
Investiture Conflict, marked the first breach in the notion of
Christian unity. It was from the concealed depths of this fissure
that the slow decay of the Middle Ages was to spread.[3]

---

[1] A few examples may serve to illustrate the process; in the Frankish period
killing in battle was not considered to be a sin but merely a stain, for which forty
days of penitence had to be observed.   In 955 the German army against the Hun-
garians fought under the flag of St. Michael, Warrior of God. From the late tenth
century onwards church benediction became more frequent in the knighting ceremonies—' in the protection of churches, widows and orphans '. The Cluniac
Reforms helped the process along; the warriors of Pope Leo IX in the battle against
the Normans (1054) were called ' milites Christi ', and the fallen were regarded as
martyrs—in spite of Peter Damian's impassioned protests against any use of arms
by the church. The concept of ' holy ' war finally triumphed when it was invoked
by the Gregorian party (i.e. in an internal church quarrel, not in war against the
heathen!); the troops of Gregory VII were called ' militia S. Petri '. Then, as a
result of the appeal of Urban II, the First Crusade was undertaken in the spirit of
an armed pilgrimage (with indulgences, etc.), and was a complete success. Finally,
a kind of clerical knighthood was proclaimed in the *De laude novae militiae* of Bernard
of Clairvaux, which was dedicated to the religious orders of knights then being
formed.

[2] A. Meyer-Pfannholz, ' Die Wende von Canossa ', *Hochland XXX* (1933),
385 sqq.

[3] For the above, cf. Cl. Frh. v. Schwerin, *Germanische Rechtsgeschichte. Ein Grundriss*
2nd edn., Berlin, 1943); O. Brunner, *Landschaft und Herrschaft im Mittelalter* (2nd
edn., Brünn/Munich/Vienna, 1943); C. Erdmann, *Die Entstehung des Kreuzzugsge-
dankens* (Stuttgart, 1936); E. Eichmann, *Die Kaiserkrönung im Abendland* (2 vols.,

These are only a few, but perhaps the most significant, examples of the process which is usually called the ' Germanization of Christianity '[1]—the twin, complementary process to the Christianization of the Germanic world. That such a process could have happened only among primitive, undeveloped peoples is fairly obvious. The age had set itself an ideal and could see no means of attaining it other than by such anomalous methods.

The new age was still ignorant of the potentialities of life and of the world. It knew nothing of the complexities and conflicts which appear, even in religious matters, when standards of thought and culture become more demanding. Hemmed in by its own narrow horizons, having no first-hand experience of the world, the mediaeval mind could accept the ideal of Christian faith as a feasible, attainable objective, once it had opened its mind to it. To this ideal it dedicated itself naively and optimistically. The first, decisive hurdles were cleared with a youthful *élan* which brushed aside all inhibiting doubts as to whether there were perhaps stars in the sky to which human hands could never aspire.

The numerous, fervent attempts to attain this ideal, which were continually renewed through the Middle Ages, cannot be recounted here. The Germans, being more fully committed to it as a result of their close connexion with the *Imperium*, pursued it with great tenacity, and came nearest to realizing it. But, as the horizons of life widened, the chances of success of a programme which regarded so many complicated features from one point of view only became more and more tenuous. In practice, at least, the Middle Ages were gradually forced to recognize the distinctions arising out of different aspects of life and society, each having different standards. The later Middle Ages, having become more prudent and more moderate, were content to let the once absolute scale of values lose its clear, firm outlines.

Würzburg, 1942); P. E. Schramm, *Herrschaftszeichen und Staatssymbolik* (Schriften der Monumenta Germaniae Historica XIII, 1953); A. Dempf, *Sacrum Imperium* (Munich/ Berlin, 1929); G Tellenbach, *Church, State and Christian Society at the time of the Investiture Contest*, transl. R. F. Bennett, (Oxford, 1940); R. Foltz, *L'idée de l'empire en occident du 5e au 14e siècle* (Paris, 1953); G. Barraclough, *The Mediaeval Empire. Idea and Reality* (London, 1950).

[1] Cf. H. Böhmer, ' Das Germanische Christentum ', *Theologische Studien u. Kritiken* LXXXVI (1913), 165 sqq.

In the early and mature Middle Ages the very nature of Christianity and culture made men regard them as identical and co-extensive. Both universal culture and Christian culture resulted from a unique constellation of historical factors which could never appear again. With this in mind, we are perhaps even justified in giving the inadequate term ' Middle Ages ' a positive meaning. It could be used to signify the period which stands as an intermediate age between an epoch which had not yet arrived at such a conception of the world or such a pro-gramme of culture, and an age which no longer took them into account.

THE CLASSICAL INHERITANCE

Almost all that we have considered up to now has revolved around the fundamental question of the new epoch's relationship to its inheritance from the Christianity of the ancient world.[1] It is obviously a complicated problem and warrants one final attempt to elucidate it. The first, and essential, point is that the ancient world in its decline had regressed to forms of material and spiritual life which provided a very favourable basis for the subsequent amalgamation with such native assets as the young peoples of the north possessed. In the political sphere, for example, the disintegration of administrative institutions within the Roman Empire, in Italy and Gaul, opened the way for the introduction of a feudal system, although its political functions were still very limited and primitive.

The economic and social structure was characterized by an extensive system of *latifundia*—self-supporting estates based on serfdom and slavery. The rise of the self-supporting estates was accompanied by a radical reduction in trade and industry. Both the spiritual and the primitive trends in religion, which included what there was of philosophy, converged into the main stream of transcendental otherworldliness, however this concept was interpreted (see above, p. 4 sq.). Creative art went the same way in both form and content, as we shall presently show (p. 51 sqq.). These developments represent what B. Schweitzer has recently called the ' pre-mediaeval Middle Ages '.[2] This was the only

[1] For traditional Germanic elements in the Middle Ages see below, p. 51 sqq. and p. 72 sqq.

[2] B. Schweitzer, *Die spätantiken Grundlagen der mittelalterlichen Kunst*, 6.

basis on which the Middle Ages could assimilate the inheritance of the ancient world. The ancient world and the Middle Ages met half-way, or, at least, they leaned over to meet one another.

This is so obvious that much recent research has inclined to the view that the transition from classical antiquity to the Middle Ages was a smooth, unbroken development with no significant breach of continuity in either material or intellectual life. This was the view, in particular, of A. Dopsch and his followers. But this argument ignores the immense vacuum in all intellectual things from the sixth century to the eighth, which is marked all over the continent and which separates the period of the creative powers of the old world from the time when the new epoch started to display its potentialities. Admittedly, a tenuous thread of continuity cannot be denied; but it had become as feeble and ineffective as a trickle of water in the desert, which may disappear at any moment. In reality there was a well-marked caesura between the two periods.[1]

This situation left a legacy of serious consequences for the Middle Ages proper—or at least for the first half of the epoch. What are the facts of this dependence on the ancient world? All historians underline as one of its most obvious characteristics the fact that the epoch was completely dominated by the ideas of ' tradition ' and ' authority ', implying that it clung desperately to its prescribed inheritance. That was just how the period saw itself! All through the Middle Ages thousands of cases were settled by confident appeals to the wisdom of the past. The reputation of having copied the 'Ancients ', particularly the early Christians, was no reproach against a writer—on the contrary, it assured recognition and respect for his work. For ' the works of our forefathers are in all ways excellent; nothing new can evermore be created—God hates reformers '. This belief was still

[1] For this section, cf. A. Dopsch, *The Economic and Social Foundations of European Civilization* (London, 1937); A. Dopsch, *Die Wirtschaftsentwicklung der Karolingerzeit* (2 vols., 2nd edn., Vienna, 1921); H. Pirenne, *Mahomet et Charlemagne* (3rd edn., Paris/Brussels, 1937); R. S. Lopez, ' Mohammed and Charlemagne: a revision ', *Speculum XVIII* (1943); E. Perroy, ' Encore Mahomet et Charlemagne ', *Revue historique CCXII* (1954); R. Latouche, *Les origines de l'économie occidentale, IVe–XIe siècle* (Paris, 1956); H. Aubin, *Vom Altertum zum Mittelalter*; *Absterben, Fortleben und Erneuerung* (Munich, 1949), who admits only a very limited continuity; and J. Spörl, ' Das Alte und das Neue im Mittelalter. Studien zum Problem des mittelalterlichen Fortschrittsbewusstseins', HJB. L (1930), 279 sqq., 498 sqq.

affirmed by a canon of Liège in the late eleventh century. It was only thereafter that voices began to be heard warning against this uncritical equation of the old with the good and the new with the bad. One of the first was Otto von Freising, who arrived rather precociously at the conclusion that the passive conservation of a stage once reached is impossible, for 'man must pine away unless he receive fresh sustenance for his growth'.

This thesis of a Middle Ages hemmed in by the tradition and authority of antiquity is fully justified. But the antithesis that there is a beginning to the Middle Ages is equally important. This beginning is marked by a clear break in the continuity of intellectual tradition, in philosophy and in experience of life. Such a break was essential before a new period could emerge. The break made it possible, or at least much easier, for the new period to dispose so freely of its faded inheritance, to adapt it to its own thoughts and feelings and yoke it to its own will and ambitions. It was only in this sense that the Middle Ages really assimilated that which was handed down to it.

Besides the examples given above (p. 22 sq.) the mediaeval appreciation of Augustine, revered as the supreme Father of the Church, is an excellent case in point. His lofty speculations, springing from a restlessly probing intellect and fired with a compelling power of dialectic, were naturally far above the unsophisticated mediaeval mind. It was so much easier to comprehend Gregory the Great! Consequently men restricted their attention to the apologist and moralist in Augustine along with what was, or appeared to be, practicable and attainable in his work. Peoples just serving their intellectual apprenticeship could do nothing with the spiritual message of the *Civitas Dei* which soared above all the works and institutions of this world, including the church on earth. It had to be transformed to represent the idea of the factual reality of Christ's rule over everything on earth before they could grasp and accept it as a programme to be applied.[1] It has been shown above how the philosophical otherworldliness of Boethius' *Consolatio* was tacitly commuted into a renunciation of the world in the sense of

---

[1] Cf. H. X. Arquillière, *L'Augustinisme Politique. Essai sur la formation des théories politiques du moyen-âge* (Paris, 1934).

Christian asceticism. Furthermore, Gregory the Great was regarded throughout the Middle Ages as the perfect model of a Pope, and nobody could have been more insistent than Gregory VII that his example alone should be followed. But what is there of the restraint and wisdom of the author of the *Regula pastoralis*, whose first concern even as Pope was to proclaim the duties of the ordinary pastor to be the ' art of all arts ', in the severity and arrogance of Gregory VII's *Dictatus papae* and in his other hierocratic manifestoes with their emphasis on rule and power?

The view that ideas were the property or copyright of the discoverer was alien to the Middle Ages, and men were indifferent to scholarly accuracy when it came to interpreting the facts of tradition. This led them into a blind acceptance of any interpretation of vital matters which was favourable or congenial to their views. Without the slightest burden of conscience they were prepared to help things along with pious deceit, and even with blatant forgeries, when nothing else would work. Both the Donation of Constantine and the Decretals of Pseudo-Isidore were at the roots of numerous bitter disputes and claims in church politics for centuries to come, and were used in scores of cases where the interests of a monastery or a bishopric were at stake. Facts were acceptable only when they were according to plan, and what was in the plan had to be translated into effective reality at all costs. The only reservation was that facts that could not be denied had to be justified through the words of an ancient authority as quickly as possible. Thus the German College of Electors had scarcely made its first appearance as a fully constituted body, about the middle of the thirteenth century, before its foundation was attributed to Charles the Great. Nevertheless, the mediaeval mind was not so completely devoid of critical ability as appearances might lead us to believe. But wherever there was a clash between what they saw and what they wished to see, the result was a twilight outlook which, for our understanding, is one of the most difficult features of the mediaeval mind. For this reason we should not be too hasty in passing moral judgements on the Middle Ages.

Besides the tendencies which led to an approximation between late antiquity and the early Middle Ages a few opposing or extraneous factors must not be forgotten. Even the Christian outlook of late antiquity inevitably had many features which were out of place in the new period, although this was perhaps never fully realized at the time. The cult of tradition and authority handed down to the Middle Ages was derived from the wisdom and caution of ripe old age, typical of a disillusioned world, saturated with experience and totally uncreative. Friction between this heritage and the self-assertive, untapped energy of the new peoples, which was greatly increased by the successes which led to the foundation of the Carolingian Empire in 800, was almost inevitable. However much the period may have fallen under the spell of ancient classical civilization, it is doubtful whether ascetic scepticism and renunciation of the world, either in a philosophical or in a purely religious form, can have played a really dominant part in this young and vigorous epoch. There was no room for the resigned attitude expressed by such phrases as *nos homunculi in fine saeculi* or *saeculum senescens*. In the Middle Ages men did not simply resign themselves to the impending end of the world. The weary frame of mind for which it was a virtue that ' even in his youth his heart beat like that of an old man ', as Gregory the Great claimed for St. Benedict,[1] cannot have been typical. The Middle Ages as a period was far too restless and vital to adopt these views to any significant extent. There is plenty of evidence that this façade of idealistic other-worldliness barely covered an extremely practical and realistic approach to the business of this world, not only in secular society but also in monastic circles. We need only call to mind the insatiable pride of possession and love of acquisition of religious foundations. It is significant, for example, that it was in the highly ascetic Cluny that a comprehensive, centralized financial administration (*camera*) was developed, which was transferred almost immediately into the Papal Curia during the reforms at the time of the Investiture Conflict. Such deep-rooted anomalies

[1] Although E. R. Curtius (*European Literature and the Latin Middle Ages*, 98 sqq.) has shown that the ' puer senex ' is an old literary ' topos ', ' originating in a particular outlook of late antiquity ', it does not justify the assumption that the Middle Ages adopted the idea thoughtlessly, without investing it with a serious, intended meaning.

constitute both the strength and the weakness of the Middle Ages; they are the source of many great achievements and also the reason why the period was unable in the end to keep pace with its problems.

THE PATTERN OF THE PERIOD

The central, governing theme of mediaeval history is, then, the subordination of all earthly attributes to a purely clerical design—at least in principle—and the succeeding process of emancipating them step by step. As a consequence a common, western European civilization was formed, which developed further until it included every aspect and form of culture, and set the standard both for the individual and for the community as a whole. It was like a mighty process of breathing in and breathing out, lasting over a thousand years, in which the breathing organ was represented by the other-worldly, clerical system of values, which first inhaled what was left of a tottering civilization, then transformed it according to its own exigencies and finally, either voluntarily or under pressure, restored it to independent life breath by breath. Goethe recognized long ago that this was the basic phenomenon of all life.

I. The first phase of the process, representing ' breathing in ', lasted from about the beginning of the sixth to the middle of the eighth century; in this period the foundations of the Middle Ages were laid. After this the period falls into the following phases, at least in broad outline.

II. The common culture of European Christendom occupied the three hundred years from the Carolingian Renaissance to the end of the eleventh century. Whatever elements of culture had been admitted into the clerical scale of values and had survived under its protection the great crisis at the end of the ancient world, were organized, applied and encouraged within the limits of the religious order of things. They grew into a unique, all-inclusive pattern, whose monumental outlines were most clearly defined about the turn of the millenium.

The whole of the second half of the Middle Ages represents the reaction against this pattern—the ' breathing out '. The danger from new forces just beginning to make an impression was felt even on the religious side. Their pressure from within threatened to destroy the edifice of the church, for such innovations as the dialectical method went right to its foundations. Conversely, the more conscious of their powers the new movements became the more they chafed against the superimposed values of the church. Finally, both parties came to see that their aims and methods were different, and actively sought a separation. Hitherto, as the early mediaeval theory of kingship shows, the words ' secular ' or ' profane ' had not been applied in a pejorative sense. But now the ' world ' was thrust out of the religious sphere completely. Also, as the world unfolded its scope and possibilities to men as individuals, secular society fought to regain its independence. But it must be emphasized that the secular world did not seek to throw off the Christian character with which the preceding centuries had saturated it. Throughout the Middle Ages ' secularization ' means ' de-clericalization ' and not ' de-Christianization '—apart from a few exceptional cases which, however important in themselves, are not significant for the period as a whole.

The process of ' breathing out ', i.e. the release of the world from clerical domination, falls into two distinct phases. It was not finally completed until the Age of Enlightenment in the eighteenth century!

III. First there were the breaches in the conception of a unitary civilization in the Hohenstaufen period. These resolved into the first bitter quarrel between the ascetic outlook of clericalism, which did not become really militant until this time, and a code of life and morals produced by a knightly courtoisie which was consciously secular and yet convinced of its own absolute Christian orthodoxy. In addition, the clerical circles themselves lost much of their previous rigidity of purpose; natural, cultural pursuits broke down the old barriers, mainly under the guise of intellectualism, but there was already a great attachment to pure aesthetics. At the same time new demands for personal experience prescribed new paths for religious consciousness. Every aspect of the culture of a united Christendom had started to wane.

IV. There followed two and a half centuries of disintegration. After the inspired, creative phase during the Hohenstaufen period, the later Middle Ages relapsed into an instability and indecision which almost amounted to open retreat. Secular society continued to conquer its own domains and furnished them with an infinite variety of forms and opportunities. The ascetic code, disjointed and degenerate as it was even in the monasteries, showed surprising resilience; nevertheless, people were still uncertain whether or not the true *religiosus* was represented by the world-renouncing monk. The middle classes, unlike the knighthood of the previous period, were never able to establish a consistent outlook of their own which was equally valid by Christian standards. Even the movement which we regard as the epitome of deliberate secularization, Humanism, was by no means as convinced of the unassailable truth of its ' worldly piety ' as it proclaimed itself to be. The anomaly of the Christian layman and, consequently, the problem of a Christian culture, remained unsolved. The period of the great religious revolution, which we call the Reformation, was the first to approach these confused issues from fresh points of view and attempt new solutions.

Chapter II

MEDIAEVAL WESTERN CHRISTENDOM FROM THE CAROLINGIAN RENAISSANCE TO THE BEGINNINGS OF COURTLY CIVILIZATION

1. The Carolingian Renaissance and the Formation of the Western Mind

To an extent scarcely equalled by any cultural movement in world history the Carolingian Renaissance was produced by the creative initiative, the will-power and the ambitions of one single genius—Charles the Great. George Dehio, the historian of art, underlined this fact with regard to his own subject: ' Charles is the first person whose name can claim a place in the history of German (!) art; judged by the extent of his influence it is also the greatest name, for by this criterion no artist has ever done as much as this non-artist '.[1] This judgement could be applied equally well to all other spheres of civilized life. In the five hundred years which followed Charles's death no creative writer equalled, much less surpassed, the influence of this man, whose preoccupation with plans for culture and education almost amounted to an obsession—although he himself could not write!

Charles's cultural achievements had their roots in the universality of the empire which he established. The hub of this empire lay in the lands between the English Channel and the Lower Rhine. The *Translatio Imperii* really denotes the transference of the lead in culture to the north of the continent. It was only because he was ruler of an empire which even contemporaries regarded as the embodiment of *cuncta pene Europa*, only through his position as *caput orbis*, that Charles was able to bring together in the school and academy at his court an intellectual *élite* previously dispersed and isolated in all the lands of Europe. Through the same central power the Germanic peoples were drawn out of the segregation of their individual cultures and set to work together towards a common end.

[1] G. Dehio, *Geschichte der deutschen Kunst* i, 31 sqq.

The main founders of the new movement were: Alcuin the Anglo-Saxon (d. 804), the director-in-chief of the new education; the Visigoth, Theodulf of Orleans (d. 821); the Lombards, Paul the Deacon of Montecassino (d. 799) and Peter of Pisa (d. *circa* 795); the last three represented the direct contact with the culture of the Latin Mediterranean. To these must be added the West Franks, Modoin (d. after 840) and Angilbert (d. 804), and the East Frank, Einhard (d. 840). In the west, at the court of Charles the Bald, Lupus of Ferrières, one of the most important figures of the Carolingian Renaissance, was outstanding among the younger generation. In the east Alcuin's work was carried on by his former pupil at Tours, Hrabanus Maurus (d. 856), abbot of Fulda and archbishop of Mainz, who, as ' Praeceptor Germaniae ' was responsible for the incorporation of Germany into the new educational system. In this task he was helped considerably by his own pupil, Walahfrid Strabo of Reichenau, who died at an early age in 849.

Tribute must be paid to the preliminary work of the numerous wandering monks from Scotland and Ireland, starting about the end of the sixth century (Columbanus, the most important of them, died in 615), which made the foundation of the Carolingian Renaissance doubly secure. From the turn of the seventh and eighth centuries it was particularly the Anglo-Saxons, led by Willibrord (d. 739) and Boniface (d. 754) who continued this missionary work, and did so much to revive religious and cultural life in the heathen and dissolute Frankish realm. The isolated islands of Britain had cultivated some vigorous young offshoots of antique Christian culture at a fairly early date and these were not damaged by the conflicts which disturbed the continent. They eventually developed to fruition in the type of the universal scholar represented by the Venerable Bede (see above p. 12). It was from these islands, and not so much from the motherland of Mediterranean culture, which had itself degenerated into crass barbarism, that the renaissance of north-west Europe began. Paradoxically, it was this influence from the far north-west that led to the assimilation of Germanic Europe into the cultural orbit spreading from the Mediterranean south. This was the fundamental contribution of Britain to the formation of a common

culture of the west. There was much Iro-Celtic influence on the
continent of Europe in succeeding centuries—the rich, inexhaustible imagination which sustained the plastic arts and the
courtly romances of the mature Middle Ages, for example—
but its greatest contribution remained the work of conversion.
And so, although the Carolingian Renaissance did not start
absolutely from scratch, it was nevertheless unique in that no
cultural movement before or since has been distinguished by a
programme of such consistency, vision and determination.

Its outer forms and aims are well known: reform of the
alphabet and the language, tireless philological effort to produce
purer texts of surviving works, in particular the Bible, and, above
all, renovation of the whole range of education according to the
prescription of the Seven Liberal Arts (see above p. 13 sqq.). After
the barbarism of the Merovingian period these measures were
absolutely imperative as a preparation for the return of the west
to effective intellectual, ethical and aesthetic standards. All
future culture in Europe built upon these foundations. To appreciate this it is only necessary to remember that but for the work of
this period our knowledge of Classical (Latin) literature would be
scanty in the extreme, and that all our modern scripts, including
the so-called Gothic or 'black letter' and modern German writing,
are derived from the Carolingian Minuscule.

But what motives lay behind these plans for a new culture?
Are they explained by Modoin's well-known lines: *Rursus in
antiquos mutataque saecula mores. Aurea Roma iterum renovata
renascitur orbis*? Does this imply merely renovation—a renaissance? Alcuin formulated the programme much more explicitly
in a letter to Charles the Great. 'If there were many men like
Charles himself a new Athens would arise in the land of the
Franks. Indeed, it would be even more distinguished than the
old, for it would be ennobled by the *magisterium Christi*, surpassing
all the wisdom of academic philosophy. The old was illuminated
only by the Platonic disciplines and instructed in the sevenfold
arts, but the new is enriched in addition by the sevenfold blessing
of the Holy Ghost, and is thus superior to all worldly knowledge.'
So, more was intended than a mere 'rebirth' of something that
had passed away. The aim was to transcend, to surpass, the culture

of the ancients; to complete the work of the classical world. Men felt they could do this because they had a share in the monopoly of truth held by the Christian faith.

Alcuin explained that God is the highest, inexhaustible Good, the *summum* of beauty and the fount of all happiness. There is the germ of a *naturale lumen scientiae* hidden in the human mind, but just as a spark must be struck out of the flint with steel, this natural source of light must first be made to burn by the efforts of the teacher. It is simply a different metaphor for Socratic ' midwifery '. It is in the nature of man that he shall recognize and love God as the *summum bonum*. The study of learning ' beautifies and enhances the soul of man '. The soul finds ' all-surpassing peace ' in the pursuit of learning, and comes to a happy fulfilment ' because it is in the image of the supreme Trinity '. Just as the truly good makes man happy, evil makes him unhappy. This does not mean to say that the things of this world are bad in themselves, but merely that, according to the old philosophical dictum *ne quid nimis*, man must make use of them with care and in due proportion. Hence, provided that the ultimate objective of *summum bonum* is kept in mind, wisdom may even be sought for its own sake. This was asserted by Lupus of Ferrières as well as Alcuin. Similarly, the cultivation and appreciation of intrinsic beauty—*the elegantia sensuum* of Lupus—is one of man's prime obligations. For aesthetic appreciation leads the mind up to those divine levels from which all beauty proceeds. Both Alcuin and Hrabanus Maurus insisted that the arts lead on to the virtues, in particular to *sophia*, and the many talents exercised in them are gifts of the Divine Trinity.

In the opinion of these scholars, although the ancients definitely failed to arrive at complete truth, they did achieve a very high standard in philosophy and literature through their *naturale lumen*. Virgil might, indeed, in Alcuin's words, be a falsifier, but his authority cannot be despised. ' Beneath the surface of the untruths, which are particularly frequent in these poets' fables about the gods, a great deal of truth lies concealed ', says Theodulf of Orleans; but, he adds, ' learned Christians frequently are able to transform these falsehoods into truth '. The ancients could not be ignored as though they were obsolete

and finished with. Hrabanus regarded them as indispensable
mentors in wisdom, and particularly in eloquence (*sermo decorus*),
which brings joy to men's hearts. But now, their strivings and
attainments, which could never achieve fulfilment in paganism,
could be fulfilled and perfected in the ' modern ' world.

Such opinions gave these men a strong feeling of elation and
a new self-respect. Although the premonition of living in the
last days of the Christian world is always with them, the old,
timid attitude of the *aetas decrepita*, as described in the so-called
Fredegar at the beginning of the seventh century, was completely
overcome.   Instead these Carolingian poets raised once more
' high-sounding songs, which shall not be forgotten so long as
the sun fulfills its journey on its fiery steeds . . . or so long as the
icy waters of the sea shall boil . . .' (Modoin).[1] Both Alcuin and
Hrabanus Maurus asserted that there was no longer any need to
bow before the songs of Linus or Orpheus or Virgil!

Certainly, harsh comparisons were made, such as Alcuin's
between the ' Lies of Virgil ' (*Vergilica Mendacia*) and ' The Truth
of the Gospels ' (*evangelica Veritas*). A few men of this epoch were
not altogether proof, particularly in their old age, against moral
qualms and doubts on the subject of uncritical admiration of the
heathen poets and the value of worldly learning; both Alcuin and
Einhard and even Lupus are examples. Such conflicts are as old as
' Christian Humanism ' itself. Augustine and St. Jerome experi-
enced them, but they soon found a solution for the dilemma—a
solution used repeatedly throughout the Middle Ages, to which
even fifteenth-century Humanists returned. Through a typically
arbitrary, allegorical interpretation of certain biblical passages
(Exodus iii, 22 and Deuteronomy, xxi, 12) they came to the
conclusion that it is not only permitted to Christians, but even
required of them to adopt the treasures of the heathens and put
them to their own service. In fact a knowledge of the ancient
writers was necessary to understand Holy Writ (see above p. 15).
Alcuin said that it was also helpful in defending the Christian faith
against its enemies. Even if it was only an excuse for a Christian

---

[1] The fact that such images are, naturally, borrowings from antiquity should not
be used as an argument that the feelings expressed are not genuine. Cf. the note
above (p. 30) on *topoi*.

conscience which could no longer deny its hunger for beauty in the only form which it knew—namely that of classical civilization—the fact remains that the occasional scruples which were expressed could not change the general admiration of Carolingian society for classical antiquity.

If men were to achieve a higher, more refined culture the models of classical antiquity were absolutely necessary. It would be a very distorted picture of the Carolingian Renaissance which left the impression that it was only an ethical, religious movement with a garnishing of humanistic learning and directing its efforts only to the most remote regions of the beyond. On the contrary it embraced and affected human life as a whole. Its leaders were equally stimulated by both intellectual and sensuous enjoyment; their company is redolent of cheerful good humour and the comforts of this life. Earthly and profane questions were not suppressed. The Academy and the Round Table of Charles the Great cultivated all aspects of a richly developed, lively social intercourse. Their conviviality was grave, trivial and humorous in turns—and at times their humour could be very coarse. There was even a place for the uninhibited sensuousness of the classical plastic arts; Theodulf of Orleans, at least, had no inhibitions in this respect. As Lupus admitted to Einhard, the prospect of honour, fame and reward at the hands of the Emperor also stimulated their enthusiasm for study and poetry. This passion for poetry could scatter all anaemic theorizing to the winds and take complete possession of a man. (*Viscera tota tibi cecinerunt atque capilli*, as Alcuin wrote of a poet who died young; elsewhere he uses similar words about himself.) Even if their poetry and correspondence were almost entirely devoted to theological and clerical matters, it was far greater in quantity than the output of succeeding centuries. It shows the widespread enthusiasm for writing in an age determined to show what it could do. Their letters, whether in verse or in prose, show a strong feeling for the value of individual personality. An intensive cult of friendship not infrequently led to an excess of sentimental feeling in which physical and spiritual love were merged. On the other hand, the spiritual value of heterosexual love does not seem to have found its way into their writings.

Even the secluded cell of the cloister lost much of its ascetic severity. For Alcuin it had become ' a sweet, beloved residence ', surrounded by the blossoms and the fresh shoots of fruitful nature, where the teacher with holy mouth explains the books of wisdom; where, at the fixed and proper times of day, monks raise their joyful voices in ' holy praise of the Thunderer ' (*laus sancta tonantis*); and where the boys' sacred songs ring out through the halls . . . . The power of man's intellect and the purity of his heart were, for him, proof that he possessed a nobility which he could never lose. He was not merely an insignificant part of the world, for he, and he alone, was made in the image of the Creator, and God was his salvation, his light and his glory. According to a hymn by Alcuin (and there are similar expressions in Hrabanus Maurus), man must praise and love Him, who, as *mitis et pius rector in orbe*, rules the world and the fate of man. The sworn enemies of this world, with their elaborate measures to eliminate the body and the most innocent earthly longings, had little to say in Carolingian Christianity. These dismal ascetics and hermits who could never perform sufficient extravagant acts of piety in their efforts to secure canonization, were rare. This is evident in the lives of a number of saints of the ninth century. They convey a calmer, better balanced outlook, which had no need of such dubious means to prove their Christian piety. Their religious conscience *lived* in them; they really felt at home and secure in the divine protection and were confident that they had a firmly established place in God's order.

All things considered, Christian Humanism was the ideal, in spite of all that modern scholars have said to the contrary. The practical outlook of the day and the forms of social life as well as the theoretical foundations all contribute to the same general picture. Nor is it altogether correct, as almost all works on the subject repeat, that this Carolingian Humanism was completely derivative, following the pattern of classical civilization, both heathen and Christian, as though it had scarcely a thought to call its own. It is true that Carolingian writers were seldom able to put their thoughts and feelings into words of their own; they almost always express them in borrowed terms. But the strange thing is that these borrowed clothes fit them perfectly, as though made to measure. It is hard to find a single example where they restrict the author's intentions like a strait-jacket. The same could not be claimed for all the Humanists of the fifteenth century! The Carolingians assimilated the alien material into their very beings, adapted it and made it completely their own with astonishing perception and versatility. This will be confirmed when we deal with the pictorial arts of the Carolingian Renaissance (see below, p. 56 sq.).[1]

2. THE EXTENSION AND CONSOLIDATION OF THE GENERAL FOUNDATIONS

THE FIRST PHASE OF GERMAN CIVILIZATION
(FROM THE LATE NINTH TO THE ELEVENTH CENTURY)

What may be called the ' natural ' or ' organic ' growth of a civilization proceeds in progressive steps from the simple, primitive forms in which it came to life to more richly developed, more varied forms of both intellectual and technical activity. This variety and richness reflect the multiplication of *individual* talents and powers and are the result of their interacting influences. In the case of the Romano-Germanic peoples of the north, how-ever, the peculiar features which were emphasized at the beginning of this book resulted in a reversal of the normal course of develop-ment in the early stages. The unprecedented energy which brought about the Carolingian Renaissance out of the crass barbar-ism of the Merovingian period produced a peak of culture in which only a small *élite* participated, and which was far in advance of the general state of development of the young peoples of the north. They had omitted an essential stage and had to repair this omission in retrospect.

The Carolingian movement was and remained exclusive to a

[1] For the preceding section, cf. L. Halphen, *Charlemagne et l'empire carolingien* (1947); H. Fichtenau, *The Carolingian Empire* (Oxford, 1957), particularly Cap. IV; M. L. W. Laistner; *Thought and Letters in Western Europe from 500 to 900* (London, 1939; 2nd edn. 1956); S. Singer, ' Karolingische Renaissance ', GRM XIII (1925), 187 sqq., 243 sqq.; Fr. Heer, ' Die Renaissance-Ideologie im frühen Mittelalter ', *Mitteilungen des Instituts für österreichische Geschichtsforschung* LVII (1949), 23 sqq.; H. Liebeschütz, ' Wesen und Grenzen des Karolingischen Rationalismus ', AK. XXXIII (1950), 17 sqq.; E. S. Duckett, *Alcuin, Friend of Charlemagne* (New York 1951); A. Kleinhausz, *Alcuin* (Paris, 1948); E. v. Severus, *Lupus von Ferrières* (Bonn, 1940).

small group of scholars and aesthetes in touch with the court.
There was no question of it producing an educated class of any
significant proportions. Equally, its relatively ambitious, humanistic theology, and even its attitude towards piety, had left the
capacity for religious experience of the average contemporary a
long way behind.[1] The whole movement gives the impression
of a carefully planned, tended and protected garden surrounded
by rank, virgin wilderness. Within this garden everything was
controlled and directed to a given end according to definite
ideas of order, proportion and limits—as is the case with every
' Humanistic' movement. In addition, the culture which it
took over and adopted was not only foreign but also highly
developed and very intricate. The average intelligence of the day
was quite incapable of participating in it. As a whole the Carolingian Renaissance was an over-exertion; it over-reached its
powers in quantity and quality. From this basis no further progress along the same lines was possible. It was necessary to
harden-off the tender greenhouse plant—which meant that it had
to slow down its growth, become stronger, hardier, and at the
same time, coarser and less complicated.[2]

Furthermore, the centre which produced the Carolingian
Renaissance lay in the western territories, which for centuries
had been saturated with Roman traditions. In this area it retained
its impetus much longer (possibly the reign of Louis the Pious
is an exception), with the court of Charles the Bald as its focal
point. But the difficulties involved in adapting this culture to the
less congenial lands in the eastern half of the Carolingian Empire,
which were for the most part free of Latin influence, were greater.
Many a rarefied product of that protected western garden either
withered away or had to be radically distorted and restricted in
the process. The work of Hrabanus Maurus is a very early
example of this; Walahfrid Strabo is clearly another instance (see
above, p. 35.).

---

[1] Hauck stresses the fact (*Kirchengeschichte Deutschlands* ii, 146) that it had scarcely
any influence on the practical efforts of the average priest, nor, in consequence, on
the religious outlook of the people in general.
[2] The social and political troubles of the Carolingian Empire in decay were, of
course, largely to blame for this; but the inner, intellectual development, which we
are attempting to explain here, seems to be more important.

The period from the late ninth to the mid-eleventh century was spent not in creative progress but in conserving and further assimilating what had already been achieved. Past achievements were set on a broader basis, in forms which could be more widely understood and more generally attainable. Everything became simpler and less pretentious; one might even say that it smacked more of the schoolroom and had a ' home-made ' quality. At the same time it was more genuine because it repre- sented so much better the potentialities of contemporary society *as a whole*. This period, not excluding the incorrectly named ' Ottonian Renaissance ', belongs to the honest, straightforward, average man, a type just as essential to the success of any civiliza- tion as the impatient, progressive intellectual. During this period, also, the still unformed and inchoate outlook of the Germans had to be harmonized with the civilization of the south, in such a way as to produce a specifically German way of life and thought out of the more general Romano-Germanic characteristics of the Carolingian period. The only immediate, positive results of this process during the period were in the field of the pictorial arts (see below pp. 51, sqq.), where progress was most impressive.

None of the German rulers of this period had anything like the initiative or ability of Charles the Great. This was certainly true of Otto the Great; and Otto III, who died at the age of twenty-one, never reached the fullness of his powers. Naturally the royal court was a source of inspiration in many ways, but there was no longer a centralized control and co-ordination of all intellectual and artistic activities, as there had been at the Caro- lingian court. Henceforward the scene was dominated by the great monastic houses and the schools attached to them, such as Fulda, Hersfeld, Corvey or Gandersheim in the north, St. Maximin near Trier in the west, St. Emmeran in Regensburg, Tegernsee (rebuilt after the Hungarian attacks in 978), and more important than all others, St. Gall and Reichenau in the south. Even during the transition from the Carolingian world St. Gall produced Notker the Stammerer (d. 912), especially famed for his hymns and sequences, elegant in form and showing a remarkable warmth of feeling—the first composer of German descent. Then, also in St. Gall but a century later, came Notker the German (*Labeo*, d.

1022), whose efforts to make the basic material of an alien culture available to his students in the German tongue give him a unique distinction in this period (see below, p. 75).

In the eleventh century Reichenau produced possibly the only man in Germany whose talents and interests were as universal as those of the great figures of the Carolingian Renaissance. Perhaps he can even be considered to have surpassed them in his astronomical and musical achievements. This was Hermann the Lame (d. 1054), celebrated in the *Annals of Augsburg* as ' The Wonder of Our Times '.

In the abbeys, which had been endowed with very wealthy estates, men were interested in the affairs of the world and all aspects of civilization, in spite of the sober gravity of monastic life. Their way of life was comfortable and tolerant, but seen from the purely monastic standpoint it included some rather dubious features. There is a charming and vivid description of cloister life in the *Casus s. Galli* by Ekkehard IV of St. Gall (d. 1060). But in his case it reflects a longing for the ' good old times ' as he watches them being destroyed by completely different, new-fangled ideas originating in Cluny (see below p. 46 sqq.).

From about the middle of the tenth century the cathedral schools began to rival the monastic schools. Most of them were founded by bishops in the Ottonian period, such as Bruno of Cologne (d. 965), Ulrich of Augsburg (d. 973), Wolfgang of Regensburg (d. 994), Bernward (d. 1022) and Godehard (d. 1038) of Hildesheim, and Meinwerk of Paderborn (d. 1036). These men managed to combine their religious duties to their flocks and their political service to the empire with active encouragement of all kinds of cultural and material progress. They are the most representative types of common European Christian civilization at its best. It was due to their tireless work that it was soon possible to acquire the same grounding in the Seven Arts (even if the degree of thoroughness did vary from place to place) throughout the German kingdom. There were the cathedrals of Magdeburg, Bremen and Hildesheim in the north, Cologne, Liège and Strassburg in the west, Regensburg and Augsburg in the south. Bamberg, in the east, was founded by Henry II in 1007. The relatively few teachers at these schools known to us by name have little significance as individuals; and the few foreigners, such as Stephen and Gunzo of Novara, who came north in the days of Otto the Great, have even less individuality. They are merely the purveyors of an essentially anonymous, common type of education.[1] The demand once made by Hrabanus Maurus among others was almost realized: ' There must be no difference between the several nations, for the one catholic church extends over the whole earth and all the faithful are equally sons of the Light. . . '. As far as inevitable differences in temperament and talents would permit, such a community of Christian outlook, both among nations and among individuals, was achieved without either conscious effort or a programme.[2]

ASCETICISM

Nevertheless, although the other-worldly values of the church were accepted without question during the period as a whole, two main trends in the interpretation of these values can be discerned. One current tried to attain the common goal via humanistic studies, the other by a more or less strictly ascetic denial of earthly values (see above p. 21). The first really ' puritanical ' reaction against the optimism and the cosmopolitanism of the Carolingian Renaissance set in immediately after the death of Charles the Great with the monastic reforms of Benedict of Aniane (d. 821). Even abbeys such as the *augia felix* of Reichenau were influenced by this hostile attitude to learning. ' My superiors here do not approve of my writing poetry; all forms of study are declining into a contradiction of themselves and the light of learning is unpopular and becoming rarer ', was the complaint of young Walahfrid Strabo. The incompatibility of the world and the cloister was reduced to an astonishingly simple formula; in

---

[1] Outside Germany there were a few isolated exceptions, such as the quarrelsome, self-tormenting Rather of Verona (born in Liège, died *circa* 974), or the vain and arrogant cynic, Bishop Liutprand of Cremona (died *circa* 970); but the very strangeness of their extravagances only serves to reinforce the point that there was a type representative of the times. Moreover, the form of their education was the same as that of all other scholars.

[2] For the above, cf. R. Holtzmann, *Geschichte der sächsischen Kaiserzeit* (2nd edn., Munich, 1943); K. Beyerle, *Die Kultur der Abtei Reichenau* (2 vols., Munich, 1925); J. M. Clark, *The Abbey of St. Gall* (Cambridge, 1926); W. v. d. Steinen, *Notker der Dichter und seine geistige Welt* (2 vols., Berne, 1948); A. M. Königer, *Burchard I von Worms und die deutsche Kirche seiner Zeit* (1000–1025), (Munich, 1905).

the words of Smaragdus, abbot of St. Mihiel on the Maas (d.
circa 830): ' There are warriors of this world and soldiers of
Christ [i.e. monks]—the former are liable to everlasting torment,
the latter are given eternal life after death '. According to Bruno
of Querfurt (martyred by the heathen Prussians in 1009), there
are only three things which can guarantee a man eternal salvation:
the monk's cowl, the hermit's hut and the martyr's death.

It was not that this life should be regarded as part of the burden
of eternal damnation; rather as the radical ascetics saw it, it need
not be taken seriously: it was not essential to a Christian. The
ideal was to carry the Christian and Benedictine concept of
humilitas to the extreme of *abiectio sui*, to push it to a contemptuous
abnegation of all spiritual and physical human existence. This is
directly contrary to the Carolingian conviction of the dignity of
man as the *imago Dei*. These are probably extreme examples but
they vouch for a definite tendency.

L. Zöpf has said that the increase in recluses and hermits,
all indulging in the most refined methods of self-chastisement, in
the tenth century was ' like an epidemic '.[1] There was no satisfying the demand for miracles by both living and dead saints, nor
for accounts of visions, whether of heaven or hell. The tremendous wave of ascetic renunciation of the world which rose in the
tenth century was swelled by the great agent of reform which
dominated the next few decades—the Cluniac movement. All
mundane activities of body and mind were attacked. The dis-
gusting descriptions of the human entrails and their functions,
which Innocent III later made so much of in his tract *De miseria
humanae conditionis*, to illustrate the pitiful misery of man's physical
life (see below, p. 69), had largely been anticipated in the works of
abbot Odo of Cluny (d. 942). In fact, the theme had been broached
long before by Boethius (see above p. 7) and it is even to be
found in Notker the German. The harmless Virgil appeared to
Odo in a dream as a vessel of great beauty containing nothing
but poisonous snakes—the teachings of the poets! And if in spite
of everything a monk of Cluny had need of one of these heathen
books (for even there they could not be entirely dispensed with!)
he had to indicate this during the enforced silence which lasted

[1] L. Zöpf, *Das Heiligenleben im* 10. *und* 11. *Jahrhundert*, 94.

almost all the day by scratching his ear ' as dogs are wont to do, for it is not unjust to liken a heathen to such an animal '.

Still, it was only in the western parts of the Empire, in Lorraine and Burgundy, that this anti-worldly outlook assumed the proportions of a movement. On the right bank of the Rhine it was represented rather by individuals or small groups of people who might be described as professional ascetics. In particular the great imperial bishoprics and monasteries were successful in opposing it until well into the eleventh century. But even there surreptitious influences had some measure of success. The attitude of Bruno of Cologne, the main representative of the humanistic trend, towards classical studies can be taken as fairly typical of the whole period. His biographer says of him: ' He carried his library with him everywhere, like the Ark of the Covenant, and was always equipped with both the sources and the means of study: Holy Writ as his sources and the heathen writings as the means '.

It is obvious where they drew the line against classical culture. They retained the authors of antiquity as much-prized, indispensable aids to formal education, but they frigidly ignored the content and teachings of these authors. This forced them to take on an air of timid restraint. Few traces remained of the impulsive vigour in creative work or of that deeply felt appreciation of the beauties of the ancient authors which made the foreground of the Carolingian Renaissance so lively. This was as far as their ' humanism ' went. They aimed at writing a smooth, faultless Latin, and in this they were as successful as any previous age. They were eager to put the Seven Arts to full educational use, but they showed no real urge to go any further. The impulse to show off their own talents in original literary productions, to equal the 'Ancients' in their own field, had shrunk to very modest proportions compared with the tremendous enthusiasm of the Carolingians for turning out poems and letters.[1]

---

[1] It was an obvious distortion of fact, produced by extreme local patriotism, which here and there (in Liège, Bamberg, Regensburg) led them to revive the ambitious Carolingian claim to be a ' second Athens ', or, as in Paderborn, which had very few real claims to eminence, to be always ready to sing the praises of their own school. There was little to justify this. Such a man as Gerbert of Reims (Pope Sylvester II, d. 1003), a truly humanistic scholar of the Carolingian type, is naturally different—but he does not belong to the German sphere.

There was a great demand for hagiography and history in the form of chronicles. The latter had been encouraged by the political rise to power of Germany. For the rest, this period is poorer in literature and more insipid—even in its theology—than any other epoch of the whole Middle Ages. There is no sign of new life being infused into literature until considerably after the turn of the millennium, and in Germany the first attempts were much more tentative than in western Europe. These stirrings are the first faint harbingers of an entirely new period, and so belong to the next chapter. For the time being there was no attempt to progress beyond receptive learning—assimilating the traditional material of education.[1] Even in the case of the most clearly defined literary personality of the period, Hrotsvitha of Gandersheim, the first German poetess, who died some time after 986 aged about forty, the decisive characteristics fit into this pattern in spite of outward appearances. Although she made use of the drama, a literary genre which had decayed in late antiquity and which even the Carolingian Renaissance had not revived, her plays were never intended to be produced. Since their rediscovery by the Humanist, Conrad Celtis, who published them in 1501, they have been called ' comedies ', which is not quite accurate. She openly confessed a great pleasure in her own work and had a healthy sense of her personal importance, as shown by the manner in which she translated her own name into Latin *Clamor validus Gandersheimensis*, in spite of all her protestations of modesty. Terence was her model, and her aim was to use his suave style (*dulcedo sermonis*) to help her to preach Christian thought and ethics. For as she herself states many good Christians preferred the writings of the heathens to the Scriptures because of their finer language. She applied all the devices of her model with refreshing skill, and was particularly adept at introducing humorous figures and comic situations. A number of her scenes are almost ' piquant '. But what was her Christian morality like? It consistently preached renunciation of the world, extending to uncompromising preservation of virginity, rather than marriage, in order to gain the highest award, the martyr's crown. A favour-

---

[1] For literature in the German vernacular and old Germanic survivals see below, p. 73.

ite theme was repentant conversion from a sinful, dissolute life to strict seclusion and self-chastisement in a hermit's hut. For Hrotsvitha a secular life as an equally possible or equally justified Christian existence was simply not conceivable. The same ascetic, elevating aim, which was natural enough in her lives of saints, also predominates in her comedies. In form her work is humanistic, but her outlook on life is far from humanistic, for it is an essential element in the definition of humanism that it attaches great importance to worldly life and activities. Hauck described the so-called Ottonian Renaissance as ' a wedding of the education of Antiquity to the Christian spirit ',[1] but Hrotsvitha shows clearly that this definition is applicable only in a limited sense.[2]

Byzantine Influences

One further particular question must be mentioned: the relations between Byzantium and the West. Two different civilizations, both highly developed and far superior, the Byzantine and the Islamic, represented the eastern sphere in contrast to the infant culture of western Europe. Here we need consider only the Byzantine (for Islam see below p. 63 sqq.), which radiated the more important influences at this time. The Byzantine Empire was in a position of considerable strength on the continent of Europe itself; it still controlled Italy from the south right up to the gates of Rome. Nevertheless, research to date has managed to give us only an approximate idea of its significance for the lands north of the Alps.

It would appear that it transmitted some knowledge of the Greek language to the centres of the Carolingian Renaissance; in particular there are traces of this in the circle around the West Frankish King, Charles the Bald (840–877). But there was probably only one man who really knew anything about the Greek mind—Johannes Scotus Erigena (d. *circa* 877), the most inde-

---

[1] Hauck, *Kirchengeschichte Deutschlands* iii, 307.
[2] For the preceding section, cf. J. Narberhaus, *Benedikt von Aniane* (Munich, 1930); O. Dörr, *Das Institut der Inklusen in Süddeutschland* (Münster, 1934); L. Zöpf, *Das Heiligenleben im* 10. *und* 11. *Jahrhundert* (Leipzig/Breslau, 1908); E. Sackur, *Die Cluniacenser in ihrer kirchlichen und allgemeingeschichtlichen Wirksamkeit* (2 vols., Heidelberg, 1892–94)—essential; K. Hallinger, *Gorze-Kluny* (2 vols., Rome, 1950–51)—with a full modern bibliography; Guy de Valous, *Le Monachisme Clunisien* (3 vols., Paris, 1936); and J. Evans, *Monastic Life at Cluny*, 910–1157 (Oxford, 1931).

E

pendent and original thinker of the whole epoch. It is significant, however, that his pantheistic Neoplatonism, which he got mainly from Dionysius the Areopagite, was never understood by his own times. Its first real influence was on mysticism from the twelfth century on. In the tenth century there are a few isolated references to the study of Greek, but we must not read too much into these claims. Bruno of Cologne is said to have engaged ' Greek ' teachers, but they were most probably south Italians; Duchess Hadwig of Swabia is said to have been ' excellently educated in the knowledge of the Greek language '. The Empress Theophanu and her son Otto III, who considered himself ' Greek by birth ', naturally brought Byzantine ways to the imperial court—but that was only a relatively short episode. The radical asceticism, brought north from southern Italy in the first half of the eleventh century by Nilus, friend of Otto III, had a much stronger influence, but with time it merged into the general ascetic movement which spread from Cluny throughout western Europe.

It was undoubtedly the field of art that was most affected by Byzantine influence. There was probably never any interruption in the importation of Byzantine luxury goods in metal, ivory and glass; and native, European production of such things became increasingly influenced by Byzantine style and motifs. But both civilizations may well have acquired these features from their common inheritance from late classical traditions. There is very little evidence of work actually executed in Germany by artists from Byzantium or southern Italy. One example is the Chapel of St. Bartholomew in Paderborn, built in 1007 *per operarios graecos*. Its structure, a large, vaulted hall with slender pillars and richly decorated capitals, contrasts strongly with the local Romanesque style (see below, p. 54).

On the whole this eastern influence recedes considerably after the middle of the eleventh century. The schism of the churches and political enmity after 1054 were partly responsible, but the main reason was that the native development of western civilization led away from the Byzantine style. The few details of this influence which were left behind are worth noting. Love-stories and romances of travel and adventure, which were very popular

in Byzantium, found some response in the West; their influence
is to be seen in the poem *Ruodlieb* (see below p. 79) and in the
poems of the wandering minstrels (see below p. 88). The plastic
and pictorial arts of the twelfth century retained some Byzantine
elements, but they no longer consisted merely in that hieratic,
two dimensional style which we tend to regard as the essence of
Byzantine art. They show a feeling for Classical Greek form,
which at this very time was enjoying a renaissance in the Eastern
Empire.

On the whole these details do not seem to amount to much.
Varied though Byzantine influence may have been, it was merely
a case of one civilization borrowing from another material which
was suitable for and congenial to the contemporary mind and
taste. What is said below (p. 64 sq.) in principle about the adop-
tion of foreign elements is also very applicable to this case.[1]

ART AND ARCHITECTURE

To estimate its intellectual powers on the basis of the literature
which it left to posterity would be to misjudge this period's
intellectual ability very severely indeed—perhaps more severely
than any other period in history. Particularly in the reigns of the
Ottos and the first two Salian emperors, men were still too
uncertain and inhibited in both word and thought to be able to
leave any adequate account of their own characters and ideals.
On the other hand they learned very quickly to master the
irrational idiom of pictorial art. In this they attained so much
that the period has a claim to be at least the equal of the most
brilliant epochs of western art.

Art was spared one obstacle with which other cultural pursuits
had to contend. Contrary to the situation in philosophy, theology
and literature, there was no traditional, binding authority controlling art in the early Middle Ages. This is remarkable and no
convincing reason for it has so far been put forward. Artists

[1] Cf. A. Vasiliev, *History of the Byzantine Empire* (latest edn. 1952); L. Bréhier, *Le
Monde Byzantin* (3 vols., 1947); K. Krumbacher, *Geschichte der byzantinischen Literatur*
(2nd edn., Munich, 1897); H. Gelzer, *Byzantinische Kulturgeschichte* (Tübingen, 1909);
S. Runciman, *Byzantine Civilisation* (1933); J. Ph. Fallmerayer, *Byzanz und das Abend-
land, Ausgewählte Schriften* (Vienna, 1943); J. Ebersolt, *Orient et Occident* (2 vols.,
Paris, 1928–9).

continually aimed at bettering the products of their predecessors, at making their works *in meliorem ut prius statum decoremque*, and they were full of pride when they could think that they had achieved this. Consequently, the native genius of the peoples of northern Europe was able to develop more freely in art than in any other sphere of culture. Even their art was founded on the models of Christian antiquity, but the elements derived from this source were so completely fused into the native Germanic ideals of form and content that the art of this epoch can be regarded as an independent, genuinely new style, which, at its best, shows no signs of incompleteness or immaturity.

This is all the more remarkable when we consider that this mastery was achieved within a few generations and that the medium of art was even more foreign to the early Celto-Germanic north than the other expressions of higher culture. It was still foreign to them to any effective degree until well into the eighth century. The northern peoples had to evolve new forms and new themes to solve the two main problems demanded of them before they could take advantage of the models of Christian antiquity. In architecture they had to find a more substantial substitute for their own very transient and artistically limited buildings in wood. They had to learn to erect stone buildings which would be representative, monumental and designed to survive the centuries. In pictorial and plastic art they had to change from abstract, geometrical line-ornament and weaving-patterns to the representation of man—the most sublime subject for an artist, because it is the most intellectual exercise he can undertake. This second change called for an immense leap forward from one world into another, which G. Dehio justifiably called ' one of the greatest landmarks in the history of the human mind '.

1. In architecture only two main types need be considered. There was the consecrated edifice, representing a community conscious of being united in Christ—i.e. the *populus christianus* symbolized in the *Ecclesia*—and the palace of the ruler as the seat of personal dignity and political power. Of the two the latter is only of secondary importance in the peak period of the Middle Ages. Although there were attempts in the Carolingian heyday to build large and sumptuous residences for kings and emperors, as

in Aachen and Ingelheim, it was largely because the general conception of the sanctity of the Empire caused a mingling and identification of religious and secular representation. The rulers in the great days of the emperors saw the visible symbol of the power of the Empire in the cathedrals and monumental churches, which were the family monasteries of the royal dynasties, rather than in their royal residences. The Ottonians built such churches in Magdeburg, Quedlinburg and Gandersheim; Henry II in Bamberg; the three Salians in Speyer and Worms. Nothing could express more clearly that the way of life of the mature Middle Ages was founded entirely on a sense of community in religion, in which the profane was completely suffused by religious transcendentalism. The Hohenstaufen were the first to resume the practice of representing their princely magnificence by proud, ostentatious palaces—e.g. Gelnhausen, Wimpfen, Kaiserslautern. The courtly ideals of knighthood had much to do with this trend, and there is a marked decrease in the building of churches by emperors during their reigns. This is a clear sign of the first steps towards a ruling power based on and drawing its authority from secular society. The violent attacks of Pope Gregory VII forced the Empire to relinquish its sacred character and look for a source of power in secular support. The disintegration of the cultural unity of the Middle Ages around the church had already begun on a wide front.

Ecclesiastical architecture was the only kind of building in which art was involved. The standard type of church, as prescribed by Christian antiquity, was the basilica.[1] The significance of this form lies in the fact that the church restricted itself to a structure which was technically as simple as possible while yet offering opportunities for architectural expression (it could even be called ‘ spiritual ’), instead of choosing other models such as the great Roman baths with their ponderous monumentality and their showy extravagance. It was a style which the peoples of the north could manage reasonably well (see above, p. 26). At the same time the simple ground-plan of the basilica presented a

[1] Structures radiating from a central room, a style of Byzantine origin, never became popular, either north or south of the Alps, for the construction of larger churches, in spite of the palace chapel of Charles the Great in Aachen; there is therefore no need to deal with them here.

minimum of difficulties to the development of their own architectural talents.

As early as the beginning of the ninth century a development started north of the Alps which brought about a basic change in the inner layout as well as the external appearance of the old type of basilica. The richest, most perfect period of this new ' Romanesque ' style came in the last third of the tenth century and the first half of the eleventh.[1] Both geographical distribution and the amount of building done show this to have been the great period of Romanesque. Regrettably little of this style remained in anything like its original form even before the destruction resulting from the Second World War. There was Gernrode in the Harz, founded in 961, the incomparable Church of St. Michael in Hildesheim, about 1010–1030; and in the south, dating from about the turn of the ninth and tenth centuries, Oberzell on the island of Reichenau. The original design of many others, including Magdeburg Cathedral (about 960), the Church of Our Lady in Essen, St. Pantaleon in Cologne, the cathedrals of Münster, Paderborn, Mainz, Augsburg, Strassburg, Liège (all from the late tenth or early eleventh centuries), could be reconstructed on the basis of surviving original parts or other sources.

The two generations straddling the millenium were, in H. Jantzen's words, fired with ' a surpassing enthusiasm for building ',[2] in spite or perhaps because of the firm belief in the approaching end of the world! There can scarcely have been a single German bishopric and very few monasteries of any size which were not engaged in either rebuilding or enlarging or beautifying their churches. The west Frankish chronicler, Glaber (d. *circa* 1050), wrote, ' In those days it was as though the whole world was doffing its old clothes and putting on a new, shining gown . . . '.

Space permits only a sketch of the stylistic details of this new trend in art which so radically changed the whole appearance of the Mediterranean basilica. In fact, when fully developed, it

---

[1] This term, first used by a French scholar in 1820, has been generally adopted, although it has long been considered unsatisfactory. For it was the north and the north-west, Saxony, the Rhineland and northern France, which took the lead in this development. Southern Germany, in spite of having closer cultural connexions with northern Italy, was more conservative and only partly applied the new style.

[2] Jantzen, *Ottonische Kunst*, 15.

divested the basilica of its most essential features. These changes were: (1) Extension of the ground-plan to a cruciform basilica, or (as early as the ninth century) to include two transepts and two choirs in various combinations; (2) The introduction of crypts, which meant raising the floor of the choir and so interrupting the line of vision down the length of the church; (3) Sturdier pillars and columns or alternating pillar and column supporting wider arches; (4) Division of the building into mathematical proportions; (5) Externally the number of towers was increased, particularly over the crossing and as part of the west façade; the total effect of these changes was to make vertical lines an integral feature of the building. There was freedom of imagination and individual expression in the north which showed itself in a number of accepted variations without offending against the basic canons of taste and style. This guaranteed the success of the new order of architecture by contrast with the rigidly codified architectural traditions of the south. The whole development represents a progressive movement away from antique models towards a monumental, archaic style, in which abstract, mathematical principles of form are the first consideration. There is no better example of this process of leaving antiquity behind than the history of the capital. The late classical acanthus-leaf capital, a degenerate, stereotyped, naturalistic form, was employed indiscriminately during the Carolingian Renaissance, and was still used by Otto the Great in Magdeburg. Towards the end of the millennium a solid cube-capital takes its place, massive and abstract, but proportioned according to abstract mathematical principles—a genuine, nobly proportioned, archaic style. This is yet another striking example of the ' reversal of natural progress' caused by a return to a stage in cultural development which had been missed out (see above p. 41).

Jantzen called the style of the golden age of Romanesque ' an aristocratic art ',[1] and it is a fact that these imposing structures, bristling with towers and rising up like veritable ' fortresses of God ', are evidence of the aristocratic, feudal order with which the magnificence and sanctity of the Empire was so closely bound up. They are massive, heavy, material, and yet they strive upwards;

[1] *Ibid.*, 91.

they are firmly rooted on earth but their mission is to heaven. Inside, the balance and proportions of the structure are easily appreciated in spite of their lively decoration and their festive air—e.g. at St. Michael's in Hildesheim. There is no doubt or confusion apparent in them, no trace of excessive piety or ' uneasiness before God '—only the impression of a restful haven in the presence of the divine. For this aristocratic society, headed by the great bishops and abbots of the Empire, Christ was first and foremost the bearer of divine power; He was the Saviour of man and the world by His victory over death and the devil, and He was the omnipresent Prince of Peace and *Rector Mundi*. These sacred halls were the supreme embodiment of this outlook, which was expressed in a sequence from the famous collection of songs, preserved in a manuscript in Cambridge, which was probably written on the Rhine about the year 1000: *Coelo sedens, cuncta implens, factor facta continens.* . . . It was the climax of mediaeval otherworldliness, but, like all climaxes of historical development, its effective phase was very short—not quite a full century.

2. The decorative arts—illumination and relief[1]—were subject to the law of retrospective implementation even more than architecture. They began by accepting a completely impressionistic, decorative style of Hellenistic origin and finished up with an almost mystical expressionism. This latter was an archaic style of bold lines and masses, of a kind unique in the history of Western art right down to our own days.

The art of the Carolingian courts showed more contempt for the natural laws of development in its miniatures than in any other branch of art. Even the final offering of declining antiquity, the solemn, two-dimensional incorporeal, hieratic style of Byzantium (as in St. Apollinare Nuovo in Ravenna) was almost ignored. Instead they took a completely unprecedented leap in the dark—when one considers that they started with abstract, Germanic line-ornamentation—to naturalistic, impressionistic

---

[1] Only very scanty remains of the great output of wall-paintings have come down to us—mostly in Oberzell on the Reichenau. Even these give us very little indication of subject and treatment, apart from telling us that their theme was always that of Christ in His divine majesty. Statuary, whether large or small (i.e. the art of natural forms and three-dimensional masses), which had been very much neglected even in late antiquity, was so foreign to the mind of this period that only a few isolated attempts were made in this medium.

art appealing to the senses, such as had been abandoned in the antique world as early as the fourth century. Its object was to give the most natural and convincing illusion of the visible world and of man in it. This aim is quite obvious in the so-called Ada manuscript of about 800 and in the Purple Gospels of the Palace School of Aachen, written in gold on purple parchment, shortly after 800. It is impressionistic painting of a technical dexterity with which we can scarcely credit those times. The object is simply the cult of human beauty, man in this world with a mind of this world, against the background of a soft and sensitive landscape. Dehio said that these works ' forecast a new estimate of human dignity deriving from the intellect '.[1] Little more than the halo of gold indicates the reality of the world beyond, which should be the message of the ' evangelists ', whom the illuminations depict. In appearance they are more like ancient poets or philosophers—especially St. John. None the less, however much this style may tell us about the mentality and ideals of one narrow circle which worked under the direct supervision of the Emperor himself, it is only an extreme example of one particular trend. The great crop of miniatures produced in the ninth century does not follow their example, for it is usually successful in combining a subdued naturalness in aesthetic treatment with the other-worldly subject of the picture and a wealth of symbolic content.

There was no decisive change until the Ottonian period. The great school of painting at Reichenau, which was at its zenith from approximately 970 to 1020, effected in a single generation a thorough stylization and simplification of the style it had inherited from its antique models. The result was an extreme form of archaic brevity, as shown in the Gospels of Otto III, the Book of Pericopes of Henry II, and the Bamberg Apocalypses. Here naturalism is reduced to an idiom of signs and symbols. The human body represents only a frame supporting the gestures and attitudes of spiritual experience produced by divine intervention. An evangelist is seen as an absolutely incorporeal interpreter of the word of God. For the first time European painting makes use of the solemn, unrealistic gold ground.

[1] Dehio, *Geschichte der deutschen Kunst* i, 50.

Compositions which are most economical in form, yet very boldly conceived, giving an extraordinary impression of size and portent, are placed against wide, empty bands of colour. These are the means by which many of these pictures, although only in small book-format, are made to appear truly monumental.

These artists had only one aim; to make visible that invisible truth which alone is real. J. Gantner rightly called it ' an art of visionaries '.[1] Neither before nor since has any Christian art in the west succeeded to this extent in disembodying the visible and the tangible in an attempt to leave the world behind, whilst yet retaining a sense of the aesthetic values and intellectual powers of expression of which form, line, mass, colour and gesture are capable. The unknown monks who produced these works were among the most inspired artists the German people ever produced. And yet, even here the Reichenau school was an exception. Many other schools of painting—Regensburg, Fulda, Hildesheim, Cologne—were, as H. Jantzen said, ' intellectually much more restricted '.[2] But their basic intention of either rejecting or, at least, severely curtailing the influence of antique naturalism, was the same. In this they were helped by the Iro-Scottish influence coupled with a strong reversal to primitive Germanic ornamentation.

In relief-work (book-covers, liturgical utensils, bronze castings, etc.), just as in book-illumination, these two centuries are occupied by the struggle between the native urge towards archaic form and content and the ideal of realistic beauty provided by their classical inheritance. In this field also, although there is one section which shows a relatively strong desire to lean on the old traditions, the main stream of development reduces and standardizes form in the interests of greater intellectual expression, in the same spirit as did the Reichenau school in painting. Examples of the former trend are the bronze doors of Augsburg Cathedral and the Pillar of Bernward in Hildesheim. The famous doors of Hildesheim Cathedral (contemporary with the others— about 1015), decorated with pictures giving an intensely dramatic, dynamic effect in the purest archaic style, show the latter trend.

[1] Gantner, *Romanische Plastik*, 11, quoting H. Focillon.
[2] Jantzen, *Ottonische Kunst*, 97.

During this period no other country in Europe produced anything to equal these German works, either in architecture or in the pictorial arts. And there is a good reason for this. This art lived and breathed in the atmosphere of the Empire, whose ruler contemporaries regarded as *typus Christi Salvatoris,* and whom these miniatures depict as being crowned directly by Christ himself. It is nothing more nor less than the art of the Empire, with the fortunes of which its rise, climax and decay exactly coincide.[1]

[1] For the preceding, cf. M. Hauttmann, *Die Kunst des frühen Mittelalters* (Propyläenkunstgeschichte, Vol. VI) (Berlin, 1929); H. Jantzen, *Ottonische Kunst* (Munich, 1947); A. Goldschmidt, *Die deutsche Buchmalerei* (2 vols., Florence/Munich, 1929); J. Gantner, *Romanische Plastik* (Vienna, 1941).

CHAPTER III

THE FIRST SECULAR CULTURE
THE HOHENSTAUFEN PERIOD

IF it be accepted that the idea of a common civilization co-
terminous with western Christendom represents the very essence
of the Middle Ages, the golden age of the period must be regarded
as ending with the Investiture Conflict. The decisive turning-
point occurred about 1100. After this date all that had been
excluded from the concept of ' God's Kingdom on Earth ', such
as the intrinsic value of profane things, the particular and the
individual, came back on to the scene. In each of the contradictions inherent in the mediaeval world (see above p. 18 sq.) the
side which hitherto had remained passive now became active and
gradually attracted more and more life and vigour from its
opponent which had previously predominated almost unchallenged. The common forms of culture were dependent on
static conditions of life and society; now newly aroused forces
made life dynamic and creative. Every joint in the old order of
things began to gape.[1]

Political unity broke down under the weight of two powerful
rivals, of whom one rose to power on the shoulders of the other.
The Papacy was the first to declare war in the Investiture Conflict
with its hierocratic claim to wield an *Imperium spirituale* over the
whole world. Close on the heels of the Papacy came the new
national, territorial and city states. These two combined in their
ideology and their realistic power-politics to destroy the power
of the Emperor. The proud *Renovatio Imperii* of the Hohenstaufen
soon showed itself to be a tragic striving after a moribund ideal.
The violent methods—brutal even by contemporary standards—
frequently adopted by the Hohenstaufen dynasty, and the too

[1] Cf. H. Pirenne, G. Cohen, H. Focillon, *La Civilization Occidentale au Moyen Age
du XIe au milieu du XVe siècle* (Histoire générale, tome VIII, publiée par G. Glotz)
(Paris, 1941)—important and comprehensive; G. Paré, A. Brunet, E. Lesne, *La
Renaissance de XIIe siècle, Les Écoles et L'Enseignement* (1933); C. H. Haskins, *The
Renaissance of the Twelfth Century* (Cambridge, 1927); R. W. Southern, *The Making of
the Middle Ages* (London, 1953).

emphatic phrasing of their imperial proclamations, betray the concealed nervousness and uncertainty of men who are surrounded on all sides by superior enemies and are fighting for their very existence.

The common civilization of the west suffered exactly the same fate. It is the purpose of this chapter to show how this unity split up into different 'cultural climates', into different styles of mental and spiritual outlook. These all overstepped the boundaries of principalities and peoples to varying degrees, according to their natural range, and so they acted as a brake on the imminent disintegration of Europe into national units. In fact they produced a new and stronger sense of community in the Western world—the sense of a common chivalry embodied in the order of knighthood. Alongside the new order the old, monkish attitude to this life and this world was still very much in evidence; indeed, it was stronger than ever and threatened to carry off one half of the world on its crest like a huge tidal wave. But here again, as in the case of the Hohenstaufen emperors, the violent, aggressive tone of this party, with their world-renouncing avowals, betrayed that they were faced with a world which had started to change its allegiance and was already hostile.

Germany, fighting to maintain the pre-eminence of the Empire in Europe, and itself so immersed in traditional imperial theories, adhered instinctively and more closely than the other European nations to the old spiritual principles and standards with which the conception of the Empire was hedged about. She was forced on to the defensive and into the backwaters of the new trend in European affairs. The Romance peoples, at first, mainly in the west, took the lead all along the line. They had a much lighter burden of tradition and such as they had they recognized as a brake on the development of their own powers. In addition, their natural temperament was freer and more mobile, and fired with enthusiasm for progress in the most diverse fields. They showed an uninhibited, eager enjoyment of life and the things of the senses, coupled with scepticism and indifference towards anything which smacked of metaphysics—a frequent combination. Every significant feature of the new epoch was produced by the Romance peoples of the west or the south, and it was in their

lands that the new trends were most fertile and productive.[1]
The primitive Christian sincerity of the Waldensian or Franciscan
preaching of poverty; renunciation of the world and the body,
which was darkly ascetic and partly a Manichean heresy; the
intimate sensibility of early Mysticism; the analytic scholarship
of the new learning, of Dialectic, Averroism, and Scholasticism,
which were represented in the institution of the University—all
these were products of western Europe. In the sphere of influence
of the school of Chartres, which extended throughout north-
western Europe, including England, they fostered a humanistic
admiration for the beauty and greatness of the heathen culture of
antiquity. They discovered an enthusiasm for the inexhaustible,
life-giving powers of nature, which they hid under a very thin
coat of religious varnish. Their Gothic art strove to cast off the
burden and the trammels of earthly existence. They evolved the
way of life of secular knighthood, with its lofty aspirations, a *nova
militia Christi* embodied in the military orders, and a great enthusiasm for the Crusades under the slogan 'God wills it'. In
contrast with this first concern of Christianity, war against the
infidel, their sober middle classes practised a calculating devotion
to business.

The more conservative and ponderous German temperament
was slow and cautious in accepting these stimuli from the west,
but it did try, nevertheless, to assimilate them into its own character and outlook. Its main concern was to iron out the crass discrepancies which were obvious in the new material and to reconcile it with the old emphatic distinction between this world and
the world beyond. Above all, it was essential that the unity of
all aspects of existence should be maintained.

Albertus Magnus (d. 1280), the only German among the
really great representatives of the new learning, proved his
greatness as a thinker by combining Neoplatonic penetration
with Aristotelian accuracy of definition in his philosophy and
theology. He united abstract science with empirical methods of

---

[1] Not all the Romance peoples had an equal share in this, of course. The lead
was given, on the one hand, by northern France and middle and northern Italy
(areas which, although they were thoroughly Romanized, were characterized by a
relatively strong Germanic racial admixture) and, on the other hand, by the purely
Mediterranean south of France.

observing natural phenomena, and was also remarkably sensitive to the problems involved in contemporary developments of state, society and church. Albert observed the world not only from the seclusion of the scholar's desk; he sought to comprehend and influence life in all its robust reality. It is precisely in this respect, in co-ordinating different, or even contrary approaches, that he shows his superiority over the theorists and systematizers of Romance scholasticism—with the possible exception of St. Bonaventura.

It was quite natural that the Germans should be the first to produce a great literature which gave complete, and in many cases permanently valid, expression to the new self-awareness of lay society. In doing this the Germans, led by the creative urge of their brooding earnestness, gave expression to certain profundities and problems of life which were never revealed to the Romance peoples. Even in intellectual and spiritual matters common to both races there was already a distinct cleavage between the different national characters.

THE INFLUENCE OF ISLAM

There is one particular reason for the general ascendancy of the Romance peoples at this time. It was the influence of Islam, the second great cultural power after Byzantium, which penetrated into Europe through Romance lands. Naturally, the waves of Islamic influence lost their effective force the further they proceeded from their point of origin.

Mohammedanism as a world power stretched from Spain across north Africa well into the continent of Asia, and reached a brilliant peak of cultural development between the ninth and the eleventh centuries. The contemporary western world could boast no intellectual or material achievements of anything like the same quality. During the Crusades western eyes were opened in amazement—and they coveted what they saw! They saw a rich and astonishing variety of the material attributes of a more refined standard of life. There were costly textiles for clothing, carpets and elegant furnishings for living quarters; they had weapons of very high quality; they were skilled in the use of spices, medicaments and cosmetics. The enjoyment of good food had led to the cultivation of a wider range of vegetables than the west had ever dreamed of. The code of honour and the class-ideals of the noble Arab knighthood corresponded closely to their own principles and ambitions. Finally, all intellectual pursuits were allowed the widest scope; the library of the Khalif of Cordova is said to have contained close on 400,000 manuscripts.

It was from Islam that the West got the *complete* Aristotle—it came in the first place from Spain in the form of an Arabic adaptation, and shortly after in translation from the original from the Byzantine-Arabic enclave of southern Italy. Along with Aristotle they obtained a great variety of works on medicine, natural science, including astrology and geography, and a great deal of esoteric, mystic speculation of Hellenistic-Oriental origin on the mystery of the universe and the place of the human soul within it. And there was poetry (love-lyrics) besides other kinds of literary work. The main impact was made by the fact that there was nothing close and narrow about the intellectual horizons of Islam. The rigid absolutism of their tabulated, dogmatic religion was constantly at strife with their free philosophy, whose aims were the limits of human perception and a more complete appreciation of life in general. The representatives of the latter trend were by no means free of enlightened scepticism, religious indifference, or even pessimistic resignation. This world with which the west now became acquainted glittered with all the colours of the rainbow, it was exotic and flamboyant, and, most surprisingly, it was a heathen world. Little wonder, then, that closer acquaintance with it only helped to undermine the European's feeling of security and immutability in his own intellectual —and even religious—world, and suggested to him some very searching questions concerning its finality. Even though we cannot assess these influences in detail, there is no doubt about the great importance of the sum effect of Islamic culture on the Western world of this period. It must be borne in mind that, in all cases of different civilizations influencing one another, only such features are echoed and adopted as find a congenial, responsive element in the receiving civilization. The many different ways in which the culture of antiquity was accepted and assimilated throughout the centuries of the Middle Ages show this quite clearly. What the Middle Ages discovered was always what they were looking for and what they could understand. This applied to the Byzantine influence in Europe (see above p. 49 sqq.), just as it applied to contacts with Islam.

Although the Crusades brought mediaeval Europe into closer and more regular contact with the Islamic East, they had long had some acquaintance with it. Charles the Great had connexions with the Caliph of Baghdad; even in the earlier Middle Ages the pious custom of making pilgrimages to the Holy Land, both as individuals and in small parties, was not unknown; and sea trade with the adjacent ports of Asia Minor and North Africa, particularly via Venice, had been revived in the ninth century, since when it had grown enormously. But in those early days the western mind could make little of a heathen civilization, however cultured and refined it might be. Only when the Western world itself had developed a long way in the direction of a more cultured life was it able to understand and welcome the stimuli coming from the East. It would be only a slight exaggeration to say that it was not because Islamic civilization invaded Europe that the latter changed so much, but that the internal development of Europe had made it ripe for a change. It was because there were many people who were impressed by this foreign influence and ready to welcome it that Islam played such a great part in shaping the new epoch.[1]

DISCOVERY OF THE INDIVIDUAL

It opened up an immense range of spiritual and intellectual possibilities as well as new material standards. The individual in the higher ranks of society had to make a choice for himself. It was something quite new to have to refer to one's own judgement, to one's own thoughts about the true destiny of mankind in this world, and to have to decide on this or that course for the best. The individual became his own point of departure in his dealings with the world.

[1] C . C. Brockelmann, *History of the Islamic Peoples*, transl. by J. Carmichael and M. Perlemann (1949); M. Horten, *Die Philosophie des Islam* (Munich, 1924); T. J. de Boer, *History of Philosophy in Islam* (1903); S. Runciman, *A History of the Crusades*, 3 vols. (Cambridge, 1951); U. Monneret de Villard, *Lo Studio dell'Islam in Europa nel XII e nel XIII secolo* (Città del Vaticano, 1944).

F

The perceptive judgement of Bishop Marbod of Rennes (d. 1123) that a man could either ' stand there in himself ', or ' be given back to himself ' or ' let himself be drawn out of his own being ' and thereby 'lose cognizance of his own self', seems to herald a new epoch. A full century later Thomas Aquinas reduced this simple, personal experience to an abstract, scientific formula —namely, that each and every being is a unity which stands on a higher or lower plane in life according to the degree to which his words and deeds proceed directly from his true self, which is the foundation of this unity. John of Salisbury (d. 1180), the great English scholar, probably the best educated man of his century, returns again and again to this same problem—the problem of the true development of individuality, even as a way to a just and happy life in this world. According to him the greatest danger is the estrangement (*alienatio*) of man from himself, whereby he loses all ' dignity of his nature and of his person '— in other words, his personal identity. A man then plunges into a ' land of oblivion ' (*terra oblivionis*), in which he is unaware of himself, and finally succumbs to simple ' human degeneration ' (*degeneratio hominis*).

The problem was thus ethical, but naturally there remained behind it the more fundamental question as to the purpose and aim of human existence. The nature and purpose of human life became the first intellectual concern of the epoch; even the most hostile and contradictory ' schools ' had this in common. Bernard of Clairvaux asked and answered the question for his whole age: ' Think ye then that it is a little thing, to know how to live? It is the greatest of all '. The problem was bound to become crucial as soon as the individual was no longer able to get standards (real or imaginary) from a general, objective source, which provided absolute and unambiguous prescriptions. But what was meant by ' knowing how to live properly '? That was where opinions differed.

The old ascetic otherworldliness which dominated men's minds was first developed into a programmatic system in the twelfth century. This took place, in its higher forms at least, under different auspices, namely under the auspices of early mysticism. Bernard of Clairvaux (d. 1153), whose powerful personality fascinated his contemporaries as no other, ' gave a new positive content to clerical asceticism, which had previously been essentially negative '.[1] This new content was the thought of the ' imitation of Christ ', achieved by contemplation and submersion in the story of the salvation, and by the highest degree of self-abnegation.

Supported by the mysticism of the Song of Songs (Christ as the bridegroom of the soul) Bernard brought his generation to consider above all else the human aspects of Christ, saying ' Even if I am not able to preach of Christ-our-Lord, I will at least speak to mankind of Christ-the-Man ' (*saltem ipsum hominem homo hominibus loquar*). The silent worship of Divine Majesty, high above all thought and feeling, which claimed a divine victory even on the cross (see above p. 56), was transformed into devotion to the helpless Innocent in the manger, or perhaps more frequently, to the pain-wracked Saviour of the Passion. This is shown in Bernard's own hymn *Salve caput cruentatum* and, in Germany, in Frau Ava's *Life of Jesus*. Behind this devotion lay the idea of sharing the sufferings of Christ, and an emotional sense of sorrow and repentance for man's personal burden of sin, which was the cause of His sacrifice.

This, again, was an approach to the individual viewpoint and the individual will; man is exhorted to search himself for the solution, to apply his own powers to the problem. [There was also the worship of the Virgin Mother; the need for an intercessor, a ' mediator ', whose human qualities encouraged a feeling of familiarity and intimacy, resulted in her being accorded an ever-increasing importance in the process of absolution and salvation, which was completely foreign to the older theology founded on the New Testament. Enthusiastic, pious souls busied themselves with realistic, fantastic and emotional descriptions of her life on earth. Worship of Mary, praise of Mary, laments for Mary, invocations of Mary, extending from soft and tender idylls to passionate outbursts of souls in torment, came to dominate religious literature, both in Latin and in German.]

Thus the attempt to make religion a personal matter was accompanied by an equally strong effort to invest the Divinity

[1] Caspar, *Geschichte des Papsttums*, ii, 565.

with realistic, visible and tangible human characteristics. Men tried
with all their powers to deprive the divine of its erstwhile other-
worldly aloofness and take possession of it at their own, human
level. Apprehension through the senses was substituted for a
groping, visionary concept of the divine. As men's minds
developed to the limits of their natural capacities (see above
p. 19 sq.) they did not hesitate to apply personal logic even to the
most objective subject—religion. Conversely: the new approach
to religion made man more sensitive to the voices within him
with all their wide and constantly changing range of expression.
Thus the new ' individualism ' was nursed and encouraged in its
early days just as much by religious stimuli and interests as by
profane factors (see below, p. 83).

THE RELIGIOUS REACTION

What is paradoxical is that precisely this urge to make the
transcendental more earthly, realistic and perceptible was accompanied by a radical, uncompromising denial of the value of the
physical attributes of man and nature. But the new trends in
religion were directed by the most ascetic brand of monasticism,
which had left far behind the moderation of the Benedictine
Rule. The spirit of Cluny (see above, p. 46 sqq.), particularly aided
by its German offshoot, the reform movement of Hirsau, had
finally succeeded in bringing Germany under its sway in the last
third of the eleventh century. It made no difference that shortly
afterwards Cluny itself became appreciably less strict in its
demands, for the movement was stimulated afresh and became
much more effective as a result of the lead given by Bernard of
Clairvaux and his Cistercian Order.

[The figure of ' Dame World ', as depicted so often in the
art of a slightly later period, represented fully the predominant
concept of earthly life. She was always represented as having a
beautiful and seductive front, but lacerated with disease and
eaten away by horrible reptiles behind. There was nothing at all
in this world, not even a well tended park, which escaped the
harsh judgement of Anselm of Canterbury: ' It invites the
enervating pleasures of the senses, for there the degenerate
breast forbears to do no shameful deed '.] For Anselm's biogra-

pher, Eadmer, the pleasures of the five senses are ' seldom good and mostly bad ' and then with overdone casuistry he proceeds to list thirty-one different kinds of *mala delectatio*, in which two, three or more senses may combine in the enjoyment of the beauties of nature or the comforts of a life of luxury. Bernard of Clairvaux and his brother even said of their own sister, that an elegantly dressed woman is nothing more than a ' snare of the devil ' and ' wrapped-up excrement '. It was no less a personage than Pope Innocent III who explained to his contemporaries the truth about this earthly existence in a tract written just before his accession to the papal throne, the *De miseria humanae conditionis*: ' Formed of dust, dirt and ashes and, what is baser, of the most contemptible seed; conceived in sensuality, in the flame of desire, in the stench of lust and, what is worse, in the stain of sin; born to care, pain, worry and, what is more miserable, to death . . . man does all that is shameful, common and vain. He reviles God, his neighbour and himself '. Finally: ' he shall become a heap of putrefaction, riddled with pestilence, which shall stink eternally. . . .'[1]

Deliberately and categorically Innocent extended this attack on sexuality even to marriage. He could not absolutely condemn the institution of marriage, as did the Cathars in the south of France, and he admits that even married people can achieve eternal salvation, but he still attaches a serious stigma to it. He makes it quite clear that, in his opinion, marriage is relegated to the very edge of what is compatible with Christianity. Indeed, it was the general conviction of this new ' intellectual climate ' that celibacy was essential to a true Christian life. Bernard of Clairvaux forced his sister-in-law under threat of sudden death to free his brother, so that he could enter a monastery. His biographer relates that mothers hid their sons from him, and women their husbands, so that they should not fall under the saint's ' terrifying, superhuman power to command ' and become monks.

The German popular epics, *King Oswald*, *Orendel* and *King Rother*, whose authors include both clerics and laymen, although they make great play with worldly wealth and pomp, end their

---

[1] The sparkling rhetoric of the original is only faintly conveyed in translation.

stories by making their heroes, who have survived many deeds of battle and long adventures in distant lands either looking for brides or abducting them, spend their last days either in a monastery or in celibate marriage. In the case of Oswald this happens at the express order of Christ himself, so that he may resist sin and not succumb to base desires!

Didactic tracts, preaching extreme asceticism, conveyed this attitude of contempt for the world to all ranks of society. Confessions of sin, such as the Confession of Millstatt, and of Vorau, a large part of Hartmann's *Discussion of Faith*, or Heinrich von Melk's *Von des todes gehugde* (*memento mori*), written in the middle of the eleventh century were responsible for this. ' You wicked world, how you do betray us ' (*ja du vil ubeler mundus, wie betriugist tu uns sus!*) was the theme of the *memento mori*, about 1070. ' You well set up lady (*wip wolgetan*), just look now at your dead husband, how his bald pate and his feet which carried him on amorous adventures now appear; and his whole body bellying out like a sail in the middle . . .' (*fuze, da mit er gie höfslichen mit den frowen . . . al enmitten da ist er gebleet als ein segel.*) (Heinrich von Melk). All parts of the body seemed to exist only in so far as they invited scrutiny of the manifold opportunities of sinning through them; feet, knees, hands, arms, heart, tongue, mouth, ears and eyes are all mentioned in the Confession of Millstatt. For these sins man must expect ' everlasting misery/ in which he shall eternally/ cry out, Woe is me!/ as though weighed down with his own barn door/ leering with terrible visage . . . . ' (Heinrich von Melk). Life became more and more closely bounded by death, decay, sin and eternal damnation. Sin came to be seen as the normal state of man, and the normal role of the world was to encourage sin. The famous popular preacher, Berthold of Regensburg (d. 1272), in an allegorical interpretation of a passage of the Old Testament, explained to his audience that five-sixths of humanity had fallen into the hands of the devil; but there was a chance, he added, ' that I might prevail upon the devil through my preaching '.

The message of salvation, which had been the first concern of religion, was eclipsed by moralizing and warnings against sin. Everything was represented against a terrifying background of

naturalistic descriptions of human life, this ' upper hell ', intended
to evoke horror and revulsion. In the same manner as the mystics
they addressed such preachings to the individual, to make him
aware of his real condition in this life. They inferred that it was
a personal kind of sin, rather than the original sin of Adam and
Eve tricked by Satan, that was responsible for the sufferings and
death of the Saviour, and that it was up to the individual to make
good this debt in some way. Even this was sometimes regarded
as being insufficient atonement. Into the joyous message of
Christ's triumph over death and the devil, Heinrich von Melk
introduced the warning: ' I will not allow you to enter into the
kingdom of heaven, if you continue to live as dissolutely as your
forefathers of yore . . . . ' If men were to be successful in warding
off the fate which threatened them and theirs they would have to
make tremendous efforts to ' save ' themselves through additional
prayers, ascetic practices and good deeds—Heinrich particularly
recommends almsgiving and masses for the soul. They would
have to face God in all their baseness.[1] Again, this time in the
religious sphere, the individual was given a new importance and
taught to regard himself as the centre of his own world.

Even so, this trend was not such as to destroy men's faith in
the fact that they should still be saved. The classically simple
words of a prayer in the mass used at Benedictbeuern in the late
twelfth century show that there was still unshaken faith in salvation: Christ, through His humanity, ' fosters kinship between
Himself and His people, among whom the righteous are His
children and His brethren ', and in the Communion He offers
Himself for us to partake of, ' so that His limbs shall not turn
away from Him ' (*also samenot er chunescaft zwiscen im und siner
scaft, davon die rehten genoss sint siniu bruoder unde siniu chint . . . daz
im niht entwuehsen siniu lider*). Confident, faithful rejoicing like
this, however, became rarer as men worried more and more
about their chance of salvation; and from now onwards every

---

[1] Space does not permit us to explain at length the difference between the older
' doctrine of redemption ' and the nature of salvation in the ' doctrine of satisfaction '
expounded by Peter Abelard and Anselm of Canterbury. Even the theological
approach to salvation in the latter sees it as a *legal* contract between God and man—
man's sins must not exceed the value of the mercy which Christ's sacrifice gained
for him.

individual was conscious of his own burden of guilt. It was at this time that Luther's fundamental question, 'How shall I gain a merciful God?' arose to torment people throughout the rest of the Middle Ages. But the Middle Ages looked for a solution along lines which were diametrically opposed to Luther's approach.

In this blinkered pessimism the positive qualities of an active life on earth no longer seriously counted. It was purely a negative ethical code. The obvious flaw in this approach to life, even when it was watered down a little or prepared to compromise, was that it was neither attainable nor practicable. For man in a material world it was impossible both as a spiritual background and as a moral standard for everyday life. Above all, the layman was left to himself with his problems, for it was a code which completely ignored conditions of material existence, in which he had to make for himself a Christian life.[1]

THE EMANCIPATION OF LAY SOCIETY

The apparent perfection of the ascetic, clerical way of life was also a challenge to the lay society which maintained it. In the attempt to establish itself as an equal, independent cultural force secular society had first to free itself from the restrictive influences of the church and then try to formulate its own ethical code and its own way of life. So far we have not yet touched upon this question of lay society in the Christian Middle Ages, so it is now necessary to start a long way back if we are to see the developments of the twelfth century in their true perspective. The problem may be approached from several angles: the education of laymen, the cultural value of the vernacular, and the extent to which the Teutonic mind was able to understand and assimilate the imported form and content of education.

The educational efforts of Charles the Great were by no means confined to reviving antique Christian culture, although this was

[1] For the preceding section, cf. E. Vancandard, *Vie de S. Bernard*, 2 vols. (4th edn., Paris, 1910); E. Gilson, *La théologie mystique de Saint Bernard*, (1934); *Bernhard von Clairvaux, Mönch und Mystiker*, ed. by J. Lortz (Wiesbaden, 1955); W. v. d. Steinen, *Vom Heiligen Geist des Mittelalters. Anselm von Canterbury, Bernhard von Clairvaux, Abälard* (Breslau, 1926); M. P. Buttrell, *Religious Ideology and Christian Humanism in German Cluniac Verse* (Washington, 1948); St. Beissel, *Geschichte der Verehrung Marias in Deutschland im Mittelalter*, 2 vols. (Frankfurt, 1909).

naturally the first objective because it was so indisputably superior to all other models. But Charles's interest extended also to traditional Germanic material, such as popular law, heroic lays, and 'German' language and grammar. Nor did he intend the influence of his court to be as local as it actually was (see above, p. 41 sq.). His real intention was to establish a general education of his whole people on the broadest possible basis, but all the circumstances were against a policy of this kind.

Nevertheless Charles's inspiration was sufficient to produce promising first steps towards a literature in the German language: in the ninth century there was the *Muspilli* poem, the translation of *Tatian*, Otfried von Weissenburg, the great Old Saxon *Heliand*, etc. It is true that all these works were written by clerics, and all either use exclusively religious themes, or, like the *Ludwigslied*, adapt a secular theme to the purposes of the religious idea. Otfried states explicitly that his object is to drown ' the sounds of things vain and the objectionable songs of the masses '—meaning probably the old heroic poetry.

Apart from the fact that it invests the story of the Gospels with the external features of the familiar Old Saxon world, there is little evidence that the *Heliand* shows a full understanding of Christ and His mission and adapts it to the Teutonic mind, as was so long claimed for it. Only the external form of the biblical narrative shows the native background. Christ appears as a feudal lord, the apostles as His vassal knights, bound to Him by oath of fealty and a rigid system of service and reward. The background is a detailed account of contemporary Old Saxon daily life. But, in fact, it is precisely in those aspects which were once claimed as evidence of a thorough Germanic adaptation of Christianity that the *Heliand* is completely dependent on the theological traditions of early Christianity, as transmitted by Bede, Alcuin, Hrabanus Maurus and their followers. Even on the cross Christ is seen triumphant, as *princeps* and *rex coelestis*, not as the suffering ' Man of Sorrows '. The Redemption is seen as a victorious struggle with Satan for the possession of the soul of man and of all creation, not as a sacrifice for the personal sins of individuals. These features—and the representation of worshipping mankind as a *militia Christi*—are all common to the Christianity of antiquity. They constitute the theological foundations of the objective philosophy of the high Middle Ages (see above, p. 56). It was the pressure of a more subjective, emotional outlook in the twelfth century that brought about the first significant changes in this theology (see above, p. 71, fn. 1), which eventually produced the entirely different religious thought and feeling of the later Middle Ages and the modern period.[1]

The promising start which had been made on a literature suitable for laymen ceased again in the tenth century. At that time Latin, as the language of the clergy, the sole proprietors of culture, was regarded as immeasurably superior to the vernacular in its formal and aesthetic possibilities, and ruled virtually unchallenged.[2] Even the material of a Germanic heroic lay, the *Lay of Walter* (now generally acknowledged to have been written in the late ninth century, and not by Ekkehard I of St. Gall, as was previously believed), was written in Latin; and, what is more significant, it was later cast into a mould of smooth hexameters after the style of Virgil by Ekkehard IV because he was not satisfied with ' the barbaric language which had still a somewhat German flavour '. In this poem, side by side with the Germanic enthusiasm for the tumult of battle and appreciation of tragic conflicts produced by the collision of concepts of friendship and allegiance, there is a strong admixture of Christian ethics. In fact the poem almost amounts to a stern condemnation of the old warrior mentality with its unbridled self-interest. Hagen's homily on the vices of greed and vain renown brings out this element quite clearly.

Heathen, Germanic influences continued in the substratum of many legends and superstitions (e.g. the belief in sorcery) of the broad masses throughout the Middle Ages, and even down to our

---

[1] For the preceding paragraphs, cf. G. Baeseke, ' Die Karolingische Renaissance und das deutsche Schrifttum ', VLit. XXIII (1949), 143 sqq.; H. Gössler, ' Das Christusbild in Otfrieds Evangelienbuch und im Heliand ', ZPh. LIX (1935), 1 sqq.; W. Köhler, ' Das Christusbild im Heliand '. AK. XXVI (1936), 265 sqq.; K. Hauck, ' Waltharius und Erchanbald von Eichstätt ', GRM. XXXV (1954), (Neue Folge V), 15 sqq.; and K. Hauck, ' Zur Genealogie und Gestalt des staufischen Ludus de Antichristo ', GRM. XXXII (1951), (Neue Folge II), 11 sqq.

[2] One need only recall the protracted struggle which was necessary, in spite of Dante, to establish the ' Volgare ' as the equal of Latin, even during the heyday of Italian humanism.

own times.[1]   Many motives of mediaeval drama represented this continuity of Germanic heathen ritual, but they were so overgrown and distorted by features derived from antiquity and from Christian sources that they remained unrecognized until modern research, after a great deal of tedious and painstaking work, dug them out—sometimes with very doubtful justification—from the mass of material in which they were embedded.   In general it would seem that such heathen, native elements had become ' degraded culture ', and were no longer countenanced by the cultivated classes.   A certain bishop of Bamberg, who about 1060, considered Attila, the Amelungs, and ' other such monsters ' to be more important than Augustine or Gregory the Great, was notorious for the fact and regarded as an eccentric.

On the other hand, what chance was there that foreign subjects and materials inherited from the ancient world would find expression in the German language?   Notker the German (d. 1022) said that he was ' venturing something previously unheard of ' when he translated into German and provided with commentaries a number of secular school-authors.   These included Boethius and Aristotle, the Psalms and large parts of Gregory the Great's *Moralia in Job*.   The reason he gave for undertaking this work was that things which in the foreign medium can be only imperfectly understood if at all, are much easier to comprehend in one's mother-tongue.   But the only language of clerics was Latin and the layman had no interest in such things!   Wipo, the biographer of Conrad II, bitterly reproached the Germans because, as he asserted, ' they consider that it is superfluous or unworthy to allow anybody to learn anything unless he is going to be a clerk ', and he recommends the Emperor to enact a law ordering all people of rank to see that their children are instructed in worldly subjects as well as in religion.   Naturally nothing came of it.   The secular nobility might show a lively interest in family histories and land titles, when written in Latin by monks, but otherwise (apart from the interest taken, during the tenth century, by a few ladies of ruling dynasties) there was no call for secular subjects.

[1] The ' Germanization of Christianity ' caused by natural social conditions, described above on p. 22, was something quite different.

After Charles the Great's biographer, Einhard, and his grandson Nithard (d. 844), there were no secular authors until the beginning of knightly poetry in the late twelfth century. Our whole stock of written information about the period comes from clerical pens. Is it not inevitable, therefore, that our picture of the true thought and feelings of the age must be irrevocably distorted? The clergy, shut away in their monasteries or bishoprics, cannot have had the same views and opinions as responsible laymen. Nevertheless, so far as the basic pattern of life goes, we can accept the evidence of clerical documents as fairly accurate. For example, it was not merely the result of clerical imagination and contrary to secular opinion, that the sacred character of kingship and its rights and duties towards religion and the church were reiterated generation after generation in a hundred different, but perfectly explicit formulations. And again, the evidence of thousands of documents attesting the gifts of laymen to the church, stating that these endowments were made *pro remedio salutis animae nostrae*, is undeniable. It is psychologically quite impossible that all this evidence had no foundation in fact.

In addition, lay society, of which only the nobility may be regarded as being sufficiently advanced to form an independent opinion, was still virtually embodied in the clerical order of things. There were as yet no secular standards to contradict the principles established by the church; and in its turn the church did not repress but rather encouraged the pursuit of material betterment which was the main concern of lay society. It was a great advantage to be a tenant or a bailiff on a church estate or to establish and endow one's own religious foundation. The numerous gifts made to the church in the name of piety, whether they proceeded from the king or from a simple farmer, were not donations in the full sense of the word.[1] The donor was usually guaranteed some benefit by the safeguarding of certain rights for one party and the imposition of certain dues on the other. In fact, that pride of possession, which was so well developed in the primitive Germanic character, soon asserted itself again under the new conditions after the conversion of the Germanic peoples

[1] Cf. the famous article by Ulrich Stutz on ' The Proprietary Church ' translated in *Mediaeval Germany* ii (ed. G. Barraclough, Oxford, 1938), 35–70.

to Christianity. Co-operation between clerical and lay society in economic matters was one of the most important features of the early mediaeval order; later, when the church tried to withdraw from this partnership, and was successful in doing so, it destroyed one of its own indispensable supports.

But the increasing severity of the ascetic trend from the eleventh century onwards, which has already been referred to, brought a change. In the main this was a result of the general acceptance of the Cluniac Reforms supported by the movement started by Bernard of Clairvaux. Of even greater significance, the outcome of the Investiture Conflict prompted radical changes which may be summed up as a clericalization of the church. The battle cry of the Gregorian Reform, *Libertas Ecclesiae*, had treated the church (not as a matter of dogma, it is true, but very definitely in day-to-day practice) as an institution of clerics under a hierarchical rule. Thereby it deprived lay society of every right to an independent opinion in religious matters and relegated it to the role of obedient subject. Thus the balance which had been represented by the mediating authority of the king, invested as he was with functions which were half religious and half secular, was destroyed.

Gregory's claim to full dominion meant that lay society (which naturally had no share in the special sacramental functions of the priesthood within the church) was forced into a decidedly inferior position so far as law, rank, and even its economic position were concerned. In the first half of the twelfth century Honorius of Autun argued that just as Adam once begot Cain and Abel, kingship and priesthood, so Christ begot the people and the clergy of His bride, the church. Even the picture drawn by the restrained Hugh of St. Victor (d. 1141), showing the secular world forming the left-hand wall of the church and the priesthood the right, indicates clearly enough the inferiority of one class to another. The common feeling of belonging to a single *populus christianus* had undergone a serious and permanent change. The broad wedge which had been driven between clerics and laymen made the latter feel that they were indeed ' the ignorant masses ' (*tumbe laien*). It was a tense and dangerous relationship and it provided the theme which dominates the history of the late Middle Ages in every field, political, economic, intellectual and spiritual. The full implications of this development may be illustrated by the somewhat brutal statement which Boniface VIII saw fit to prefix to his Bull *Clericis laicos* (1296): ' We are taught by past history that the layman is completely hostile to the priesthood, and our experiences of the present confirm it . . . . ' (cf. below, p. 131 sqq.). There were, of course, few contemporaries who would have been prepared to go so far, but the trend is unmistakable.[1]

With Cluny and the Gregorian reforms religious other-worldliness went beyond the limits which its supporters should have found reasonable, and seriously limited its own powers of action in doing so. From this stage onwards there was no possibility of a new secular ethic combined with religious belief in conformity with the precepts of the church. Any movement towards an independent secular culture would have to find its own way without support from the church.

This was all the more important because at this very moment the higher ranks of secular society were starting to explore the pleasures and the opportunities offered to them by worldly things. They were beginning to make the most of life in the form of more luxurious furnishings, clothes, food and drink, and more refined social activities such as music, dancing, games and pastimes. All this announces the coming of a happier, less agitated and depressed attitude to life. In general this style of life started in the south of France, in Provence, and was quickly adopted in Burgundy and the north of France. A lone offshoot was soon carried into Germany from Aquitaine by the retinue of Agnes of Poitou, whose nephew, Duke William IX, was the first important troubadour. Many features of the new manner were thus brought to the court of her husband, Henry III—himself, strangely enough, one of the rulers most devoted to the dismal asceticism of Cluny. German writers, comparing the new fashion with the homely coarseness of their forefathers, disapproved strongly.

---

[1] On these changes, cf. G. Tellenbach, *Church, State and Christian Society at the time of the Investiture Contest* (Oxford, 1940); H. von Schubert, *Der Kampf des geist-lichen und weltlichen Rechts* (Sitzungsberichte d. Heidelberger Akademie, 1927); W. Ullmann, *The Growth of Papal Government in the Middle Ages. A study in the ideological relations of clerical to lay power* (London, 1955).

There was probably some connexion between these new tendencies and that extraordinary literary document, the *Ruodlieb*, the first popular novel in German literature, written by a monk of Tegernsee sometime between 1040 and 1050. It is presented in a colourful, lively fashion and shows the comfortable, self-satisfied life of a higher society of slightly lax morals. But village life also, and even the crowds of wandering vagabonds, play a surprisingly important part in it. Although the work of a monk, *Ruodlieb* is permeated with a ' free, happy state of mind ' (Manitius),[1] and its code of ethics is built on the basis of human self-control, temperance in all things (even in courage!), consideration for the less fortunate among one's fellows, politic subservience to one's superiors, and a gentle, open-minded piety.

In Germany this was only a brief interlude, which gives us a quick glimpse of the beginnings in certain limited circles of a conscious cult of courtoisie, which, however, was not fully established until more than a century later. Nevertheless, the secular side of life was showing more initiative and visibly gaining ground. Songs expressed the joys and sorrows of love called forth by the rising sap, the blossoms and the fragrance of nature. The European love-lyric had its beginnings in the eleventh century. Religious themes, particularly tales taken from the Old Testament, such as the Vienna *Exodus* of about 1100, were extensively decorated with scenes of knightly combat and other features of the familiar world of experience of the nobility. The religious drama throve on a worldly realism which was more congenial to the popular taste, but which evoked violent criticism from the more orthodox church authorities (as early as 1160). Stories from classical sources, such as the life of Alexander the Great by the priest Lamprecht, between 1120 and 1130, together with the *Song of Roland* (the first story to be adapted directly from a French source) were modernized. Such stories carried men's imagination to the distant wonders of the East, and were very attractive to knightly minds full of high enterprise and noble combat—although the dangers of excessive vanity, the subject of so many sermons, were not forgotten. Similarly the story of *King Rother* (about 1150) shows the progress towards a

[1] Manitius, *Geschichte der lateinischen Literatur des Mittelalters*, ii, 548.

fully developed courtly romance by weaving many threads of love, war and adventure into a gay tapestry.[1]

KNIGHTHOOD AND COURTOISIE

Meanwhile a new rank had been introduced into society; the knighthood was by now a stable body represented by tens of thousands of members. As a class they had risen through their own abilities from the inferior rank of *ministeriales*, and soon they acquired great political power through the part they were allowed to play in the Hohenstaufen system of government. They also profited by the respect and high reputation accorded them in general in Europe during the period of the Crusades. They were self-confident, energetic, and both mentally and materially prepared to play a very important part in the affairs of the nation and society in general. Fanatical ascetics had good reasons for directing their polemics against the knights and their undertakings, for the knights were the most eager of all classes of society to assimilate all aspects of the new secularism. They might have taken the line of Gottfried of Strassburg as their motto: ' we who are of this world ' (*Wir die zer werlde haben muot*).[2]

The way of life which the knighthood chose was precisely the one which clerical ascetics had declared to be impossible. It was ' to be pleasing in the sight of both God and the world ' (*got unde der werlde wol gevalen*)—as it was frequently formulated in the best days of the courtly period, about 1200–1210. As Freidank says, ' a happy man he, who can serve both God and the world. God makes no man do penance for being respected in this life ' (*Swer got und die werlt kan behalten, der'st ein selic man;/ got nieman des entgelten lat,/ ob er der werlde hulde hat*).

So much more was demanded of this new class than the comfortable solution of complete withdrawal from this world.

---

[1] Cf. K. Hauck, ' Heinrich III und der Ruodlieb ', *Beiträge zur Geschichte der deutschen Sprache und Literatur LXX* (1948), 372 sqq.; H. Brinkmann, *Geschichte der lateinischen Liebesdichtung in Mittelalter* (Heidelberg, 1925); Fr. v. Bezold, ' Über die Anfänge der Selbstbiographie im Mittelalter ', *Aus Mittelalter und Renaissance* (Munich, 1918); G. Misch, *Geschichte der Autobiographie, Vol. I (Altertum)*, (3rd edn., Frankfurt, 1950); *Vol. II (Mittelalter) Frühzeit)*, (3rd edn., Frankfurt, 1949).

[2] Admittedly Gottfried goes on to say ' whether it be good or evil ' (*swie so er si boese oder guot*), but he is alone in this—see p. 84.

They produced a conscious programme, the first code of morals and ideals for a lay society which the Middle Ages knew, and it was to remain the only one. It was entirely the creation of this one class and was restricted in its application to them alone.

The whole system amounted to an education for a life of rigid discipline and conventions, but one which incorporated and gave wide scope to the efforts and ideals of the knightly classes. Their true calling came first; a military conception of honour (*êre*) superseded the wild, egoistic code of the old Germanic warrior. The meaning of the word was made to conform to Christian principles, so that, from now on, honour could and must be won only through service to the weak and the oppressed, to the beloved or the imperilled woman, to the Kingdom of God through fighting the heathen, or, in the case of the German knight, in defence of the *Sacrum Imperium*.

In the code of courtly love, which represents an episode without parallel in the history of western culture, love was seen as 'the origin and foundation of all that is good' (*fons et origo omnium bonorum*). The fashion of paying court to a married woman of rank placed love and marriage in totally different categories; conjugal devotion (*affectus*) and the true (!) love (*dilectio*) of (courtly) lovers were absolutely different things, according to the French chaplain Andrew, who wrote a widely read primer of love about 1180. The main principle was that a man should educate himself, augment his personal reputation and prove his faith and constancy through untiring quests after love. These adventures had to be complicated by the most difficult conditions of fulfilment, which deliberately placed all hope of reward or success beyond his reach. But this paradoxical cult of courtly love (which cannot be traced back to either ancient classical, Christian or Germanic origins) was always the weak point in the knightly code of morals. In addition to being obviously contradictory to Christian ethics it was contrary to nature into the bargain. The subtle prescriptions of this code of love, which stylized and standardized emotion, which squeezed feeling into conventional compartments or hawked it about like a fairground curiosity, could make the most personal and sensitive stirrings

G

of the soul into empty symbols and could drive its adherents to shallow hypocrisy.

In Germany the courtly love-lyric was very popular and reached the highest standards. But this exotic genre, a ' double-entry account of love ' as H. Naumann called it,[1] came up against strong resistance in the sound, healthy German mind. All the great German masters of courtly poetry renounced it sooner or later. Hartmann von Aue and, even more decidedly, Wolfram von Eschenbach praised conjugal love; for them a man's wife was his real ' sweet mistress ' (*sueze amie*); man and wife ' spring out of the same little seed ' (*Bluent uz eime kerne gar*) (Parzival). Walther von der Vogelweide confessed to a simple, unsophisticated devotion to a lowly girl, who was the object of his love (*niedere Minne*). Most significant of all, Gottfried von Strassburg took as his theme a heroic, irresistible passion, which committed its victims to a fight for life or death.

A number of further conceptions complete the knightly code of morals: constancy (*staete*), fealty (*triuwe*), discipline (*zuht*), good manners (*hovescheit*), generosity (*milte*), noble behaviour (*hoher muot*), and happiness (*saelde*). None of these were regarded as mere gifts and talents but as tasks and duties which helped to protect the individual from all the temptations and dangers of the world. All these virtues were included in and co-ordinated by the basic virtue of temperance (*mâze*)—the middle path—which prevented any one of these virtues from becoming exaggerated and so dominating the whole personality. The knight was also expected to keep to his law of moderation in material matters, health and beauty, money and goods, importance and power in society.

Scholars have argued violently at times about this knightly code of ethics. They have asked whether, and in what way, it might be dependent on a Christian version of the moral teachings of antiquity. There were three stages of values in the antique code: *summum bonum* (*gotes hulde*), *honestum* and *utile*. The dispute is still undecided, but at all events it is impossible to deny a close relationship between these knightly ideals and the *humanitas* of antiquity.[2] Men had optimistic expectations of what the proper

---

[1] Naumann, *Deutsche Kultur im Zeitalter des Rittertums*, 145.
[2] The widely distributed tract *Moralium dogma philosophorum* or *Moralis philosophia*

guidance of moral feeling could produce and, on this basis, they
intended to remodel the life of the noble classes and make it
into a single, comprehensive system. In this scheme education in
aesthetics was as important as education in morals. Continuous
exertion of their moral will was expected to bring men to human
perfection and thus to give them the highest possible degree of
earthly happiness. All this, of course, was never more than ' the
ideal of their ambition which was not attained in reality ' (E.
Neumann).[1] In the heyday of courtoisie it was not taught to the
knighthood in the form of a dry, didactic code, but simply
through the medium of the idealized central figures of the courtly
epics, whose example they were expected to follow.

On the other hand recent research (Fr. Ranke, J. Schwietering,
G. Weber) has revealed more and more of the latent connexions
between the spiritual aspects of the courtly epic and the belief in
mystic revelation—particularly of the Bernardine type. It may
safely be said that it was from this latter source that the court
epic and presumably the knightly way of life derived their claim
to universality, their metaphysical justification and their spiritual-
ization. These characteristics distinguish the courtly literature of
Germany from that of other European countries. Certain turns
of phrase and images (the cult of Our Lady, for instance), and
typical ways of treating moods and ideas, with all their complicated language of symbols, were transferred from religious
contexts to descriptions of earthly spiritual experiences. The
effect was to sublimate and illuminate them. The whole field of
experience was brought under the influence of ' the magic world
of the heart, created and revealed by mysticism '[2] which transformed it into refined emotion. The ideas of unity in love, the
suffering and endurance involved in pain and death, perception
of the deep connexion between joy and sorrow (*liep unde leit*),

---

de honesto et utili (attributed on rather doubtful evidence to William of Conches, died
1154), a *florilegium* from Cicero, Seneca, Sallust and others, is one notable source in
support of a direct influence of this kind, particularly as the work was translated not
only into French, but also into German about 1180 by the chaplain, Werner of
Elmendorf.

[1] E. Neumann, ' Der Streit um das ritterliche Tugendsystem ', *Erbe der Vergangenheit. Festgabe für K. Helm* (Tübingen, 1951).

[2] J. Schwietering, *Der Tristan Gottfrieds von Strassburg und die Bernhardische Mystik*,
Abhandlungen der Preussischen Akademie der Wissenschaften (1943), 25.

were some notable results. Once the full implications of these
ideas had been shown they were placed on the same level as
metaphysical and religious experience. This 'secularization' of
emotion made rapid progress because it caused men to observe
more closely all aspects of the soul. The purifying and ennobling
effect of suffering is brought out when Sigune embraces her dead
lover. It is on Good Friday that Trevrizent opens Parzival's
eyes to the virtue to be gained through suffering! The final test
of worthiness for Parzival was that he should have compassion;
and indeed Wolfram's *Parzival* and *Willehalm* as well as Hartmann's *Arme Heinrich* are based on the cult of pious suffering.
They were all the result of men becoming more aware of the
inner nature of human feeling, and this itself derived from
applied religion. For the first time man's natural feelings were
given a place in Christian otherworldliness; as a result they were
generally accepted and approved, and then it was possible to
proceed to the next stage and recognize their independent existence and development. Bernard of Clairvaux's mystical *amor*, a
mixture of suffering and ecstatically inspiring love—'sufficient
unto itself, bearing its reward within itself, nor searching for any
other reason or profit apart from itself'—had its counterpart in
the concept of Love—Sorrow—Compassion which was formulated and announced by the classical representatives of German
courtly literature. But before this they had first had to move
forward beyond the cult of 'noble love' (*hohe Minne*).

Admittedly, the view that human feelings and passions were
anchored in Christian otherworldliness finds an important exception in Gottfried von Strassburg. The idea expressed by Gottfried, that noble hearts can readily fall under the spell of such a
paradoxical world of love and sorrow, life and death, appears to
be contrary to, or at least damaging to Christian teachings. This
idea is expressed by Gottfried with almost mystical ecstasy in
the prologue to *Tristan und Isolde*: 'But I would speak of another
world, which, in one heart, gathers together / its bitter sweet, its
tender woes, / its heart's love, its pangs of yearnings, / its love in
life, its death in sadness, / its death in love, its life in sadness. / To
such a life my life be pledged; / to such a world let me belong, /
and with it live or die . . .' (Tristan und Isolde, ll. 58 sqq.). The

implication is that the soul is entirely contained in this world and this life and all the inescapable tragedy of this situation is recognized and accepted. The ' goddess love ' (*gotinne Minne*) is seen as a daemonic agent of destiny; she becomes ' all powerful love ' (*diu gewaltaerinne minne*) and ' love, the supernatural power ' (*gespenstegen minne*). Tristan's love goes beyond all moral limits and becomes a law unto itself; it becomes a religion based on his semi-mystical longing to be united in love with his ' darling Isot ' (*wunnecliche Isot*), even to the extent of ' striving for an eternal dying ' (*werben umb ein eweclichez sterben*), just as religious mystics looked for their ' eternal dying ' in an ecstatic union of their souls with God. It is quite clear that it is no longer a matter of elevating the world into some transcendental sphere; the world itself has become transcendent. But Gottfried, a poet of middle-class origin, had left behind the knightly view of the world; his personal genius had led him further than his contemporaries were prepared to go. It is significant that *Tristan und Isolde* (the material is of Celtic origin) is the only tragedy among all the court epics of the best period.[1]

Men began to react to their experience of the world and secular life as they had hitherto reacted to religion; things of this world evoked the same thoughts and feelings as religious transcendentalism. And this is roughly what the courtly epic literature did for the knightly conception of life and its obligations. Just as saints won through to eternal salvation by prayer, asceticism and self-abnegation, so these model heroes of the court epic, such as Hartmann von Aue's Erec and Iwein and, above all, Wolfram von Eschenbach's Parzival, won through to absolute moral purity via long adventures, questing and straying, serving their honour and strangers in need, conscious of their own guilt and shortcomings, until they reached a noble, manly maturity. They arrived at a state of moral perfection which was given its due reward on earth—by the grace of God! Nevertheless they were encouraged to strive for perfection in a manner which differed considerably from the road to salvation prescribed by the church.

[1] Apart from the *Nibelungenlied*, which, however, derives from the Old Germanic heroic epic, and is the product of a totally different mental climate. The numerous courtly features which found their way into the Middle High German poem were not sufficient to change its essentially Germanic character.

Parzival's three ' sins ' do not fit into any church confessional, for they are sins committed unwittingly. They represent the inherent metaphysical defects in the nature of man and his incapacity to face up to the greatness and the freedom of his own heart, which is his birthright. Parzival errs and strays in mind and body; he even proclaims his defiance of God. Driven all the time by his failure to understand, he meets with nothing but pain and sorrow—Sigune and Amfortas. Finally the noble *lay* hermit, Trevrizent, convinces him of his sinfulness and brings him to accept it with humility. In this humility he is prepared to accept the high price which God demands for purity of heart and so becomes eligible to receive the mercy of God, which is dispensed quite arbitrarily and only to the completely innocent. The main point is that everything must be undertaken in a spirit of genuine penitence, without any of the external trappings of repentance, and, although Trevrizent intersperses many respectful observations about the priesthood, without priestly guidance or the sacraments of the church. It is remarkable that the specific ceremonies of the church play a very small part in the lives and characters of the heroes of Wolfram and Hartmann; they are mentioned rarely, and even then quite casually. Although the Grail derives its magic powers from the transcendental aspect of religion, it is divested of all the liturgical functions it had had in older versions of the Grail saga. Its function was simply to bestow all that one could wish for on earth (*erdenwunsches überwal*), all material comforts and peace of soul—rather like a magic lamp. But all this does not amount to a denial of orthodox Christianity, only a silently accomplished emancipation from the leading-strings of the church. The result is a faith based on human experience, springing from the depths of man's being, freeing his personality from the material debris of this life and making it possible for even an earthly existence to reach the heights.

A purely human outlook of this kind, which had developed naturally and spontaneously while remaining conscious of the ultimate limits fixed by God, was open to the influences of the noble ideals of pagan society. Purity of soul, i.e. the chastity of the heathen lady, Belakane, assumes for Wolfram the same value as baptism; and the noble humanity of Feirefiz is in no wise enhanced by his baptism. Still, they were absolutely convinced that the heathens were snared and deluded, and the war against the heathens remained for them a tragic, painful necessity. But there was a big difference between their attitude and the harsh, pitiless approach of the *Song of Roland*. For now they had come to see that the heathen also was the ' work of God's hands ' (*gotes handgetat*), as Willehalm's wife explains in a very prolix speech, adding that ' God made and holds in His hands both Christians and heathen ' (*der bede machet unde hat, den kristen und den heiden*) and that God will have mercy on them likewise. Nor did this attitude come from timid scepticism or indifference in matters of faith; it indicates the mature tolerance of the knightly ideal. They had arrived at a stage when they could understand and respect the universal and infinite love of God the Creator for every kind of noble character.

This lay piety was a combination of divine and human elements, but it was firmly based on belief in God. It is true that we to-day can only see the aims and ideals of the knightly class; we are able to define only the objectives to which a knight might, perhaps unconsciously, direct his efforts. Consequently what we have written must not be taken as representing the ordinary, day-by-day realities of the knightly ethos. Even in the literature we find many notes of depression and resignation and many outbursts of ascetic renunciation. Many of the later poems of Walther von der Vogelweide, written after he had been disillusioned by the moral decadence caused by the civil wars between Philip of Swabia and Otto of Brunswick, make this quite clear: ' World, I have perceived your reward, / you take back just as much as you give . . .' (*werlt ich han dinen lon ersehen, / swaz du mir gist, daz nimest du mir . . .*). But, for all this, the will to work towards a harmonious relationship between God and man was never impaired by such considerations. The knightly approach to life was not modelled only on the easygoing ' court of Arthur, a pilgrim's shrine of joy and courtly perfection ';[1] at its best it was capable of facing the most insoluble problems of life without losing courage.[2]

---

[1] Quoted in O. Brunmer, *Adeliges Landleben und europäischer Geist, Leben und Werk Wolf Helmhards von Hoberg* (1612–1688), (Salzburg, 1949), 85.

[2] For the above, cf. R. R. Bezzola, *Les origines et la formation de la littérature*

THE WANDERING SCHOLARS

Both Christian knights and other-worldly ascetics were very serious in their intention to ' live rightly '. But another segment of society had a totally different intellectual and spiritual approach. The Wandering Scholars thoroughly emancipated and secularized their philosophy of life without any pompous theorizing and quite independently. These vagabond clerics, wandering aimlessly from one centre of culture to another, were probably simply the product of all the unfulfilled desires and ambitions which had been dammed up behind ecclesiastical walls. When the time came they broke out with elementary vigour and spread out, uncontrolled and without direction, into the ' free ' circles of secular society.

Once they had established their position in secular society they were never tired of praising it. Their songs include a few which are so penetrating in their perception and whose linguistic elegance is so captivating that they must be given a place among the most inspired and timeless achievements of mediaeval literature—or, for that matter, of any other period of literature. The theme of love was inexhaustible for them—love on every possible note in the scales of emotion and sensation, from sweetly pathetic yearning to a coarse, naturalistic, or even openly obscene, glorification of sex. They also managed to give some aesthetic value to poems describing their rough bouts in the taverns, with endless drinking and dicing. For them nature was radiant, inviting and promising love through the glory of her springtime, and they saw her to be the eternally begetting and bearing power

courtoise en occident 500-1200, Vol. I:–1100, (Paris, 1944); J. Schwietering, ' Der Wandel des Heldenideals in der epischen Dichtung des 12. Jahrhunderts ', ZAlt. LXIV (1927), 135 sqq.; Fr. Ranke, *Gott, Welt und Humanität in der deutschen Dichtung des Mittelalters* (Basel, 1952); W. J. Schröder, *Der Ritter zwischen Welt und Gott* (Weimar, 1952); F. R. Schröder, ' Der Minnesang ', GRM XXI (1933), 161 sqq., 257 sqq.; Fr. Baethgen, ' Rota Veneris ', VLit. V (1927), 37 sqq.; M. F. Richey, *Essays on the Medieval German Love Lyric* (Oxford, 1943); B. Mockenhaupt, *Die Frömmigkeit im Parzival Wolframs von Eschenbach* (Bonn, 1941); J. Schwietering, *Parzivals Schuld* . . . (Frankfurt, 1946); J. Schwietering, *Der Tristan Gottfrieds von Strassburg und die Bernhardische Mystik* (Abhandlungen der Preussischen Akademie der Wissenschaften, 1943); Fr. Ranke, *Die Allegorie der Minnegrotte* (Schriften der Königsberger Gelehrten Gesellschaft II, 1925); C. S. Lewis, *The Allegory of Love, a Study in Medieval Tradition* (Oxford, 1936); On the problem of the code of chivalry the most recent work is: E. Neumann, ' Der Streit um das ritterliche Tugendsystem', *Erbe der Vergangenheit, Festgabe K. Helm*, (Tübingen, 1951), 137 sqq.

of life. She was ' Mother Earth, whose pregnant womb delivers its fruit . . . out of which the mass of new seed issues '.[1] But not the least part of the experience of life of the Wandering Scholars was concerned with pain and sorrow, with growing old in poverty and bitterness of heart, with their own lack of stability and direction—*similis sum folio, de quo ludunt venti* (Archipoeta) —and with the meanness and treachery of a world ruled by the whims of fortune. All this is included in their songs.

But the fundamental factor would seem to be that they had arrived at a completely objective observation of man and society without reference to moral or religious values; their philosophy is the result of simple human experience, and all that really mattered to them was an extremely mundane enjoyment of life. It was on such grounds, and not out of moral scruple, for instance, that the Primas (Hugo of Orleans, 1093–1160) repudiated prostitutes. There is no sense of relationship to God or the world beyond in their experience either of joy or of pain. Their aim was an aesthetic sublimation of the darker side of life; they accepted and defied the world as it is, just as they faced up to the mental and physical unrest of their own existence, and in doing so they drained the cup of life to the bitter dregs (Confession of the Archipoeta).

The Vagantes were fairly equally distributed throughout France, England, Italy and Germany. They counted among their numbers not only ' failed B.A.s ' or misdirected and shady characters, but also men of rank and reputation. Men like Abelard in France, Walter Map in England, and in Germany the very worldly Archbishop of Cologne, Rainald von Dassel, were closely connected with them. For the preservation for posterity of the records of their wild life we have to thank the diligent work of collection of the monks of Benedictbeuern in Upper Bavaria (*Carmina Burana*). The fact that men of rank were connected with them and that they had access to all strata of society should make

---

[1] This figure of speech is very reminiscent of the school of natural philosophy of Chartres (see above, p. 62), for the philosophy of its most typical representatives, Bernard Silvestris and Alan of Lille, was definitely influenced by heathen, antique fertility myths and beliefs. Direct influence from Chartres would be quite possible in this case; otherwise, this particular aspect of the school of Chartres seems to have had no influence in Germany.

us take the Vagantes more seriously as a sign of the tremendous vitality of the period. But they were too lacking in discipline, squandering their efforts without objective, to have any real influence on their times, and the movement soon died of a surfeit of amorphous freedom. By the thirteenth century they were almost forgotten, or at least remembered with contempt. Although the best period of knightly culture was of brief duration, and on the whole coincided with the heyday of the Vagantes, noble culture was kept alive and revived in slightly different forms by new movements (see below, p. 123), so that it remained a fruitful influence for many centuries. In comparison the episode of the Wandering Scholars was as fleeting as a shooting star.[1]

THINKERS AND REFORMERS

The main concern of the epoch was the problem of how to live—the ethical problem. But the leading minds of the time were scarcely less urgently concerned with the problem of knowledge, with the attempt to penetrate to the very essence of life and the world. Here, too, they followed widely divergent paths and arrived at completely different philosophies of life.

The preceding epoch had been able to give only stammering, fragmentary expression to its ideas on the nature of life (see above, p. 51). The ideas and the outlook on life prevalent in Western Christendom in the early Middle Ages in Europe were not adequately expressed in literature until the twelfth century. They can best be defined as ' pre-scientific ' or ' symbolistic and allegorical '. The first basic principle was that the true nature of things lay not in their own being, but that they point out a path above and beyond them to a higher, metaphysical ' something ', which shows itself only to the clerical intellect. As Hildegard von Bingen put it: ' God . . . created all material things to make known the honour of His name, showing thereby not only that which is visible and temporal, but manifesting also through them that which is invisible and eternal,' for, ' it should not be

---

[1] Cf. Helen Waddell, *The Wandering Scholars* (revised ed., 1934); H. Süssmilch, *Die lateinische Vagantenpoesie des* 12. *und* 13. *Jahrhunderts als Kulturerscheinung* (Leipzig, 1917); K. Breul, *The Cambridge Songs* (Cambridge, 1915); K. Strecker's article in the *Reallexikon der deutschen Literaturgeschichte*, ed. by P. Merker and W. Stammler, II, 393 sqq.

too much for man's acute intellect to establish a correct agreement between the visible and the invisible'. This applies also to mankind: ' Spiritual matters are expressed in apprehensible figures (*corporales imagines*), for what is said and done in a palpable manner is one thing, but the inner process to which these things point is something quite different'. (*Vita Henrici II. imp.*). All that is earthly and relative ' stands for ' (*significat*) the divine and absolute, whether it be an invisible being, a religious truth essential to salvation, or an ethical exhortation. Every tiny detail of this was taken perfectly seriously; it imposed no strain on the radical transcendentalism so typical of, and peculiar to, the Middle Ages.

Nowhere is this more clearly demonstrated than in the *Physiologus*, which after being handed down from the days of primitive Christianity in the East had been translated into as many languages as possible in many different editions, until it was easily the most widely known manual of ' natural science '. The well-known stories of the Unicorn, the Pelican and the Phoenix, all invested with symbolic, religious significance, derive from it. The rush at the waters edge signified immortality because 'the wetness in which it stands makes it always green'; or the bat represents ' in the religious sense ' the devil ' who is so fond of darkness '. And so on throughout the book. Bernard of Clairvaux regarded the stony, infertile mountains as the symbol of arrogance, but the well-watered, luxuriant valleys stood for humility, on which everything thrives. For Pope Innocent III water and blood were the most important elements in the composition of the human body, because they represent the two central sacraments, Baptism and the Eucharist. Although it was known that the features of the Man in the Moon were mountains and valleys, writers still insisted that the flecks were there to represent the sin of our ultimate ancestors (Alexander Neckam, d. 1127). One could go on citing examples indefinitely. The saying that ' things that must pass are only symbols ' was taken literally in everything they did. And the quality, merit and limitations of all material things were also assessed on the same symbolic basis.

The other basic principle was closely related; namely, that the whole universe, both natural and supernatural, from the inanimate objects of the earth to the stars from which the angels chant their heavenly music, and all that happens between them, is an indivisible unity, held together and governed by divine love.[1] Behind all this one can detect Augustinian-Neoplatonic and neo-Pythagorean theories. Centuries earlier Boethius had praised this *alternus amor*, this mutual love, commanded by heaven, as the power which 'cements the order of things, rules seas and continents', and which alone 'gives continuity to all things, for through it they flow back to the soil from which they get their being'. All visible systems are only copies of the invisible one (see above p. 23) and the structure of the macrocosm is reflected in the human microcosm. This universal whole is the stage on which 'history' is enacted, i.e. the process of salvation, which includes the macrocosm as well as mankind, and lasts from the Creation and the Fall of the Angels until Judgement Day. It was the work of Him, who, according to Hildegard of Bingen, said of Himself: ' I am the highest fiery power, who have struck all sparks of life and extinguished nothing that was mortal . . . . I blaze over the beauty of the fields, reflect in the waters, burn in the sun, the moon and the stars; I quicken all things with my breath, which is the invisible life in them'.

These beliefs led to the appearance during the twelfth century of a number of works on cosmogony and similar subjects which were intended to be text-books of knowledge of the universe, nature-lore, and world history combined. Characteristic titles were the *Philosophia mundi* of William of Conches and the *Imago mundi* of Honorius of Autun. The modern word ' world picture ' (*Weltbild*) appeared for the first time in these works—and, unlike its present-day usage, it had then a real meaning! These works were composed of semi-poetical ideas about the world and history, and although by no means exclusively German in origin, had a particularly strong appeal to the German mind. It was Hildegard of Bingen, the *prophetissa teutonica* (d. 1179), who expressed these ideas most powerfully and effectively in Germany. In towering visions, glowing with colour, she lays before us her

---

[1] All this was, of course, based on the Ptolemaic system of the universe, according to which the earth might be a disc or a sphere, but, in either case, was always at the centre of the universe.

own symbol-burdened ideas about the creation, the universe and its hidden forces, the circling stars, the elements and the winds of heaven, to which the bodily and spiritual existence of man is geared. For her the disaster represented by the fall of the angels exposed the universe to daemonic powers, but Christ, in becoming mortal, renewed the natural order of things, for He gave the soul a new relationship to God. Thus the history of the world was identified with the history of the church—the City of God standing on the slopes of the divinely controlled universe— and as such it moves forward to the end of time, when the Creator shall take back to their beginnings both microcosm and macro- cosm. In spite of all this it is quite remarkable to see how Hilde- gard, although immersed in her world of visionary revelations, manages in her writings on nature-study and on medicine to be so admirably open-minded and (in spite of all her eccentricities) displays healthy, accurate common sense in her observations of everyday life and the simple physical and mental processes of man. With such versatile interests and horizons Hildegard, who had been dedicated to life in a convent from her eighth year, proved herself to be the greatest German intellect of the century.

The symbolism of the period was concerned exclusively with the objective, impersonal elements in the whole cosmic process: naturally the problem of individual destiny was included in the wider question, but it carried no weight and was never discussed independently.[1] The same impersonal, visionary mind which expressed itself with such unique power and clarity in the works of the Reichenau school of painting some hundred and fifty years before, occurs again in Hildegard—only she expressed herself in words. They are both examples of the most thoroughbred form of the mediaeval mind in its maturity.[2]

---

[1] It is usual to describe Hildegard as a ' mystic ', but there is something mis- leading about the term when applied to her. The prime concern of mysticism— the feeling of personal union with God in the soul or the experience of complete surrender to Christ—is lacking in her works. She is quite different from Bernard of Clairvaux, for instance, in this respect. Her visions are much more prophetic than mystical in character.

[2] For the above paragraphs, cf. F. Lauchert, *Geschichte des Physiologus* (Strassburg, 1889); W. Ganzenmüller, *Das Naturgefühl im Mittelalter* (Leipzig/Berlin, 1914); H. Balss, *Albertus Magnus als Biologe* (Stuttgart, 1937); H. Liebeschütz, *Das allegorische Weltbild der heiligen Hildegard von Bingen* (Leipzig/Berlin, 1930)—a fundamental work on all aspects of mediaeval symbolism.

But, by Hildegard's time, this was no longer the only outlook on life. In fact, if we look at the development of the western intellect as a whole, we see that it was one which had almost been left behind. It shows the conservative position of Germany in matters of the intellect during the twelfth century. For Germany still adhered to a pre-scientific philosophy of this kind, whilst in the west and the south men were beginning to exercise their minds on a totally different plane. There the movement was just beginning which was to culminate in the predominance of rational, scientific thought throughout the whole world.

Bernard of Clairvaux (like all mystical, ascetic reformers) was frequently very critical of these new scientific trends. It seemed to him that it was all a matter of ' learning and learning without ever arriving at knowledge '; and he considered it to be positively unworthy ' to bring petty human sophistries into discussions of matters of faith, which are, anyway, founded upon certain, secure truths '. But it was on this point above all others that Bernard, although the greatest master of his time, was ignored and rejected by contemporary thought, even in those spheres dominated by the church. Hugh of St. Victor, who was not at all a dyed-in-the-wool intellectual, wrote the following sentence which, together with the dictum of Bernard about ' knowing how to live properly ' (see above p. 66), could be applied as a second motto to the twelfth and thirteenth centuries: ' Learn everything! Later you will come to see that nothing is wasted. There is no pleasure in limited knowledge (*coarctata scientia*) '. And Siger of Brabant (d. after 1281), leader of the Averroists, said, ' To live without learning means death and interment to any normal man '. His intention was ' to treat of natural things in a natural way '—i.e., to explain them rationally, logically. In this matter at least it seems as though the Averroists agreed with their great enemies, the Scholastics. On one occasion Albertus Magnus explained, ' In this instance we are not concerned with miracles, for now we are not discussing matters of theology but natural things '. On another occasion he said that the story of the phoenix might interest those who went in for ' mystical theology ', but there was no room for it in the natural sciences.

There is plenty of evidence that the independence of the

intellectual field, the material and methods of the profane sciences, had been fully accepted in principle.[1] Thinkers of the period had unlimited faith in the power of reason. Another leading Averroist, in Paris, stated that, ' the finest ability of man is his intellect '; and Thomas Aquinas accorded to knowledge priority over all other aspects of the soul—particularly over the will. Within a few generations this belief in reason and rational inquiry produced extraordinary successes in all branches of theoretical science and changed the whole intellectual prospect of the Middle Ages. The western world entered on its first scientific age—which was also its most productive down to the Age of Enlightenment in the eighteenth century.

This change produced some very important external consequences. The monasteries were no longer able to cater for the new demands in education, and their monopoly of learning became a thing of the past. Indeed, the monasteries which practised the Cluniac or Cistercian reforms regarded the whole movement as a threat to their aims and principles, and they emphatically renounced all participation in the rivalries of the scholars. The first result was that monastic and cathedral schools were replaced by private schools run by individual masters of the new learning, whose reputation attracted pupils from all parts. As early as the end of the eleventh century it had become customary for students to circulate from one such school to another. The mind and personality of individual scholars became more important. In fact, unless he were a saint or a great ruler, no individual could establish a claim to fame other than by some outstanding performance in the field of learning. In the larger towns (Paris came first at the end of the twelfth century) a number of school communities of this kind united in corporations which were legally independent, to form a *universitas magistrorum et scholarium* —i.e. a university. Whereas in the monastic and cathedral schools ' science ' and education had always been subordinated to religion and theology, the sole aim of the university was to cater for man's desire to learn and understand. The university was the first

---

[1] The extent to which the Scholastics developed their Aristotelian philosophy from a theological basis, or, conversely, so identified their philosophy with matters of belief that philosophy no longer counted for anything by itself, is a question which cannot be discussed here.

institution to foster this natural desire. But the development of universities in Germany was distressingly slow. The foundation of the first university in the German orbit—Prague in 1348— lagged a hundred to a hundred and fifty years behind the rest of Europe. Until then any German who was determined to have a ' modern ' education had to go, either as teacher or pupil, to other lands—to Paris, Bologna, Salerno, etc. Germany was left behind in the very field in which the period registered its most inspiring achievements. Only the *Studium generale* of the Domini- cans in Cologne was able to keep pace with the general European development after the end of the thirteenth century—and, even so, only in philosophy and theology.

Even the disciplines taught in the universities were exclusively in the hands of clerics, with some exceptions in the medical faculties. Until the days of Humanism no layman played a signi- ficant part in philosophy or theology. But even the clerics, as a class, were both unwilling and unable to turn deaf ears to the new questions with which they had been so abruptly confronted. Any confident, critical mind was free to take its choice of a number of totally different courses. One scholastic thinker, Simon of Tournai (d. 1201), is reported to have said, ' Oh, my little Jesus! I have indeed strengthened and enhanced Thy teaching in this sermon, but, in truth, if I were an enemy of Thee, with evil intentions, I could equally well weaken and disprove it with even stronger reasons and proofs '. Although this may be merely the joking remark of a self-satisfied scholar, it is a clear enough indication of the double edge at the disposal of rationalistic dialectics.

And, in fact, from their very beginnings the universities were divided and crippled by bitter academic quarrels. The so-called Latin Averroism (i.e. the movement based on the particular interpretation of Aristotle by the Arabic-Spanish philosopher Averroës), which soon predominated in the Univer- sity of Paris, amounted to nothing less than a cold, penetrating rationalism, which inevitably undermined the fundamentals of Christian faith. It denied the individuality of the soul and thus its immortality; it invalidated the concepts of free will, divine creation and guidance of the world, and eternal salvation as the ultimate aim of man. There are some signs in this system that it really aimed at complete enlightenment and maintained that the true happiness of man lies in the philosophic contemplation of truth. Hence it was possible, even at that time, to find the opinion that ' the Christian religion is a hindrance to progress in learning ' expressed in the University of Paris!

In competition with Averroism, Scholasticism as a fully developed movement, best represented by Thomas Aquinas (d. 1274), was urgently concerned with the problem of closing the widening gap between theological and philosophical truth. This was the first school of thought in Christian Europe which tried to reconcile in the same system God, the world and human life with all its ramifications. The system was constructed by a mind which was capable of both critical analysis and synthetic composition, and which was prepared to devote its powers of perception to the search for philosophic truth in the same manner as it applied them to the revelations of religion. The principles of Scholasticism were meticulously worked out in detail, and every element from top to bottom was carefully adjusted to the system as a whole. Scholastic thought penetrated and threw into relief all aspects of life and the world, the secrets of which it ' illuminated ' or ' unveiled '. In conformity with the general tenor of the age, the scholastics destroyed with reasoning the spiritualistic antipathy towards material nature. Concrete, physical things, which the symbolistic approach had deprived of all independent existence, were once more considered objectively, and their intrinsic values were again recognized.[1] Space does not permit us to describe in detail this revolution in thought. Its effects can be seen most clearly and simply in the change in the theory of dominion. Here it led to the recognition of the legitimacy of the individual national states because they were the result of natural laws and forces, and this was regarded as sufficient justification for them. There was no longer implicit acceptance of a universal and sacred empire.

[1] This is expressed in the fundamental propositions of the Scholastic theory of existence; *omne ens est unum* (individual and unique), *omne ens est bonum, ens et verum convertuntur* (they are interchangeable)—everything that exists is good and true. Naturally, this was not intended to imply that empirical inquiry should henceforward be applied to individual objects. Scholasticism at its zenith was concerned only with abstract thinking.

H

Instead of regarding reality as an 'image' of the world, grasped intuitively, men now regarded it as the sum total (*summa*) of attainable knowledge, represented by learning which could be taught and acquired. But this sum no longer amounted to an organic, self-sufficient unity as it had done in the past. Such unity had been possible only because men were not yet aware that faith and rational perception frequently contradict one another. Scholasticism was a unity based on what had been saved from the ruins of the preceding system and then carefully reconstituted. But this new system in its turn was exposed to the very force which had established its own ascendancy—namely, the restless, critical probing of the intellect, ever in search of something new. This change can be observed as early as the fourteenth century (see below, p. 145 sqq.).[1]

What, then, happened to the faith, the belief, of the Middle Ages? For obvious reasons great caution is necessary in any attempt to answer this question. Already in the eleventh century bitter religious quarrels moved an uneasy monk, Othlo of St. Emmeram in Regensburg (d. after 1070), to utter a very 'modern' sounding prayer: 'If you really exist, Almighty God, and if you are in any manner omnipresent, as I have read in so many books, may it please you to *show* me what you are and what you can do ... for I cannot endure such torments any longer!' Admittedly, this is a remarkable exception in the eleventh century, but by the twelfth century, and certainly during the thirteenth century, similar outbursts were frequent. The heretical movements of the south came north across the Alps in such strength that in 1233 an archbishop of Mainz, perhaps exaggerating a little, could say that 'there is scarcely a town, village, or hamlet that is free of this pestilence'. There were disturbing symptoms even within the orthodox church. The 'heart beset with doubt' (*zwivel*

---

[1] For the preceding, cf. H. Denifle, *Die Entstehung der Universitäten des Mittelalters* (Berlin, 1885)—Vol. I only appeared; H. Rashdall, *The Universities of Europe in the Middle Ages*, new edn. by F. M. Powicke and A. B. Emden, 3 vols., (Oxford/London, 1936); M. M. Gorce, 'Averroisme' in *Dict. d'hist.* V, 1032–1092; J. de Ghellinck, *Le mouvement théologique au XIIe siècle*, 2nd edn. (Bruges/Brussels/Paris, 1948); M. Grabmann, *Der hl. Albert der Grosse* (Munich, 1932); M. Grabmann, *Thomas von Aquin*, 7th edn. (Munich, 1949); H. Meyer, *Thomas von Aquin* (Bonn, 1938); E. Gilson, *The Philosophy of St. Thomas Aquinas* (Cambridge, 1929); Fr. A. Frh. v. d. Heydte, *Die Geburtstunde des souveränen Staates* (Regensburg, 1952).

herzen nachgebur) of Wolfram's *Parzival* was not merely a poetic fiction.

Cesarius of Heisterbach (d. about 1240) tells of the suicide of a nun because of her religious doubts; he adds, ' I could tell of many similar cases of misery, which have occurred quite recently, but it might not be good for soft-hearted people to hear or read about such things '. In 1322 another chronicler reported how the Landgrave of Thuringia, Frederick the Bold, so seriously doubted God's mercy and pity after seeing a religious play based on the story of the Wise and Foolish Virgins, that his learned advisers were scarcely able to bring him to his senses again and that his great anger lasted five days and ended in a stroke which killed him. Another recounted, about 1200, that there were many who refused to believe any longer in life after death or, indeed, in any things invisible or supernatural. The exaggerated terrors of hell and damnation, of which the preachers of repentance were so fond, missed their objective completely and produced only callousness and indifference. For, the people argued, it could not be so very bad if most of them were bound for hell whatever they might do! Berthold of Regensburg preached a whole sermon against those who held that, ' if only one is accustomed to hell, one will be just as happy there as anywhere else '— it was only a matter of getting used to it! Satires and parodies produced or stimulated by the Wandering Scholars, were widespread throughout Europe during the twelfth century, and they took incredible liberties with established reputations. They pilloried the avarice and corruption of the papal curia; they parodied the Gospels in descriptions of dissolute drinking and gambling; the Lord's Prayer, the basic liturgical texts and even mass itself, were treated with complete cynicism (*Evangelium secundum marcas argenti;* Drinkers' and Gamblers' Masses). No amount of scintillating wit could hide the bitterness behind it all. Nor can it be rendered harmless by ascribing it to nothing more than irresponsible frivolity; it signifies, at the very least, that religious feeling had been radically undermined.[1]

---

[1] Cf. H. Reuter, *Die Geschichte der religiösen Aufklärung im Mittelalter*, 2 vols., (Berlin, 1875–77)—a vast amount of material but conclusions uncritical; P. Lehmann, *Die Parodie im Mittelalter* (Munich, 1922; Parodistische Texte, XXIII); *Anglo-Latin Satirical Poets of the Twelfth Century*, ed. by T. Wright, Rolls Series, 2 vols. (London, 1872).

Averroism, as a philosophical system, naturally remained restricted to relatively small, scholarly circles and it seems to have been late in coming to Germany, where it made little progress.   Nevertheless it may have contributed in an insidious, indirect way to the general dissolution of faith and the consequent demonstrations against the clergy.   The scepticism and the tentative free thought of the court of Frederick II in Sicily, about which so much has been written, were by no means strange in the thirteenth century.   In fact, compared to some of the propositions advanced by contemporaries, many of the Emperor's aggressive questions appear childish and clumsy.

In addition to all this the Crusades turned out to be a bitter experience for Europe; they felt that ' God had left His soldiers in the lurch '.   After a minor defeat on the First Crusade, one leader is said to have cried out the threat: ' We will no longer bear Thee in mind, and none of us shall ever again trust in Thy name for help . . . .'[1] Nothing damaged the reputation of Bernard of Clairvaux so much as the abject failure of the Second Crusade (1147–49), which was instigated by him. About 1270 a Knight Templar said, ' He is a fool who would still fight against the Turks, for Jesus Christ is no enemy of theirs . . . for God, who used to keep good watch, is now asleep, but Mohammed is strong and effective . . . .'[2]

And yet we must not take all these and other similar symptoms as the definitive signature of the period.   There can be little doubt that the broad masses of all ranks remained firmly rooted in the traditional pattern of belief.   At the same time we cannot ignore these symptoms and dismiss them as insignificant.   They represent a serious crisis in religion, and they are our witnesses to the fact that the old order of the Christian church was tottering.

[1] *Cf.* A. Waas, ' Religion, Politik und Kultur in der Geschichte der Kreuzzüge ', *Welt als Geschichte XI* (1951), 225 sqq. Waas shows how these sudden fits of depression among the crusaders led them to judge the value of their religion by secular, feudal standards.   As they saw it, services rendered to their Divine Lord should give them a legal claim to the appropriate reward—when the opposite occurred this religious short-circuit was the immediate result !

[2] The whole subject is admirably treated by Palmer A. Throop, *Criticism of the Crusade* (Amsterdam, 1940).

ART AND ARCHITECTURE

In order to get to know the real character of the preceding epoch we had to make much use of its artistic products. For this new epoch this is not the case. Now there is a wealth of evidence contained in literary sources, revealing the outlook—or, rather, the many outlooks—of the period. The art of the period adds nothing to our conclusions: it merely reflects all the movements and tendencies attested by other sources.

In architecture the development from Romanesque to Gothic took place. The decisive step towards Gothic was the introduction of vaulted roof-spans, which first appeared in Germany about 1100 in Speyer and Mainz. In spite of the name ' High Romanesque ' being generally applied to this style (some do not distinguish it from Romanesque), it cannot be denied that this type of vaulting is ' the seed-germ of the Gothic style ' (G. Dehio). The implication is that the Romanesque style was changing from within. The change lent height to the interior perspectives and brought an element of dynamic contrast into the calm, placid impression of the flat-roofed basilica. The same effect was increased by a number of other stylistic features: the employment of attached columns (also used for the first time in Speyer), which, either singly or in clusters, led up from the floor to merge into the cross-ribs of the vaulting; the gradual transition from the rounded to the pointed arch; the increasing size of the windows, which led to new effects of lighting. Both inner and outer wall surfaces were treated with more imagination and were better proportioned; expanses of wall were broken up with windows and galleries. Finally, pinnacled buttresses were built along the outer wall to take the side-pressure of the heavy, vaulted roof, and in time these developed into flying buttresses with elaborate decorations. Whereas previously the aim had been to give the impression of an immovable weight of masonry, builders now wished to reach out higher, to leave the earth behind. The whole structure was given a much more dynamic character, and the interplay of architectural features responsible for this was the rather complicated result of rationalistic planning and inventive imagination. From this point of view northern France was the real cradle of the Gothic style.

But the development was slow and halting—especially in Germany. The ponderous, flat-roofed basilica was still the model for the first half of the twelfth century, as shown by the collegiate church at Quedlinburg, the Hirsau school and other examples. Vaulting did not become frequent until after the middle of the century and only became more or less predominant by the end of the century. But, although the tendency was to use more and more purely decorative features, sometimes to the extent of blurring the total impression, many massive, monumental buildings were put up at this time, such as Speyer, Limburg on the Lahn, Maria Laach. Where church building was done by Cistercians, or influenced by them, stylistic extravagances were drastically restricted. But this was for religious, ascetic reasons rather than because of artictic considerations. Buildings which we call ' still Romanesque ' or ' already Gothic ' form a wide transitional style between the old and the new, before we definitely arrive at ' early Gothic '. But by the time the rebuilding of Cologne Cathedral started in 1248, the Gothic style was fully developed and the undisputed pattern. The more energetic, more searching spirit of the new age had evolved its appropriate form of artistic expression in ecclesiastical architecture.

The main achievement in the plastic arts, however, was the rediscovery of man as a complete, living unity consisting of both body and mind. Since late antiquity (i.e. for some 600 to 800 years), this was the first attempt by European artists to master the three-dimensional techniques required for full-size works of sculpture. Almost immediately this branch of art became more important than painting; in fact the preference shewn in this period for self expression in sculpture has never been exceeded right down to relatively recent times.

This does not imply the production of independent study-figures, complete in themselves. Sculpture was still one branch of architecture, limited by the demands of church decoration and by the prescribed religious subjects.[1] Nevertheless, in spite of these

---

[1] Exceptions to this are few, but very significant: *The Rider*, in the market-place of Magdeburg (1240–50), and, especially, the *Brunswick Lion*, alive with tense, ferocious power, which Henry the Lion caused to be erected in 1166 as a forceful symbol of his power—the power not of an emperor but of a secular, territorial prince! Here, even at this early date, the intention of perpetuating his own memory

limits, the arts of the period managed to express all the different intellectual and spiritual experiences of the times.[1]

During the first half of the eleventh century the most esteemed style was of a severe, archaic type, suited to the religious purposes for which it was commissioned. Sculpture made its bow under the same patronage as painting had done before it. The bronze crucifix of Werden on the Ruhr (about 1070) admittedly expresses suffering in an idiom of primitive, poignant lines, some of which are highly decorated; but the suffering it expresses, perhaps better than any other of the countless thousands of crucifixes, is suffering defeated by divine majesty and a dignity not granted to mortals. This archaic, hieratic style seems to have been generally predominant down to the last decades of the twelfth century; an example is the crucifix in Brunswick Cathedral made in 1194. The same applies also to the other main subject of the plastic arts, the Madonna, which was then rapidly gaining in popularity. The Madonna of Bishop Imad of Paderborn (about 1060) and that of Hoven (late twelfth century) suggest purely hieratic objects of awe, having little to do with human feeling; there is nothing about them which might evoke the devotion of the worshipper, no sign of an emotional relationship between Mother and Child.

Soon, however, the spiritual animation of the period entered into art as well. At first it followed the two main courses mapped out by early mysticism; i.e. it expressed suffering, both mental and physical, and it introduced the soft, lyrical element which derives from human sensitivity. Henceforward the theme of the crucifixion was to be dominated by the *caput cruentatum*—now emphasized by a crown of thorns. The body of Christ was no longer shown *standing* with both feet planted separately on a block of wood, as had always been the case previously; the whole weight of His body was now made into a *hanging burden*, the feet *crossed* and fastened with *one nail*. From opposite sides of the cross Mary and John express the suffering of their souls, to evoke

(see below, p. 106) led him to dispense with all religious attributes and acknowledge-ments. The *Lion* is unique in this respect right down to the great statues of the *condottieri* at the time of the Italian Renaissance.

[1] The following examples cover merely a selection of a few of the most important styles, and are offered only as a crude outline. In actual fact characteristics of the different styles are inextricably mingled in the individual works of art.

sympathy in the pious spectators—as in Wechselburg (about 1230) and the western choir-screen of Naumburg (1245). In representations of the Madonna the Infant Jesus now sometimes nestles close to her body, or reaches up to her breast with innocent faith and confidence, or their heads are brought close together, so that there is an impression of intimacy as between mortal mothers and their babies. Examples of this are the Madonna in the church of St. Mary in the Capitol, Cologne (about 1220), and the relief in the cloister of St. Laurentius in Liège (about 1170–80).

These and many other pictorial themes, such as the Wise and Foolish Virgins and the Last Judgement were used by artists to convey the strongest emotions of pain, fear and despair. Their sculptures had the effect of homiletic consciences, uttering warnings that man must have a timely care for the salvation of his soul which was in great danger; notable examples are the portal of the north transept in Magdeburg Cathedral (about 1270), and the old choir-screen in Mainz (about 1240), now no longer there. The bitter arguments on the new learning are illustrated as tensely and dramatically as possible in many of the figures depicting prophets and apostles decorating the sides of the choir of St. George in Bamberg Cathedral (1220–1230). They stand in pairs arguing about the meaning of salvation. And the great church portals, decorated with statues and reliefs, are parallels to the compendia of all knowledge of the scholastics. They were a purely French innovation but soon found their way into Germany, the first example being the ' Golden Portal ' in Freiberg on the Saale (about 1230). On entering a church one saw the whole panorama of salvation, the religious history of man, represented by the juxtaposition of types of the Old and the New Testaments, of *Synagoge* and *Ecclesia*, and personifications of various vices and virtues—all leading up to the final event, the resurrection of the dead. The worshippers were forced inevitably into a mood of serious reflexion.

The awe inspired by the divine majesty, something quite beyond man's comprehension, began to diminish as the twelfth century passed into the thirteenth. The most sacred matters were now expressed in much simpler terms. But yet, in spite of the nervous tempo of the period, eruptions of feeling were always controlled by an instinctive observance of the principle of moderation (*maze*), and a certain dignity of attitude and chasteness of the spirit were everywhere maintained. It is not surprising, then, to find that most of the examples here quoted present their religious message in a more or less classic-antique form. It was still an aristocratic age![1] The shrill, gruesome naturalism on the one hand and on the other hand the overdone familiarity with all things sacred, which led people to forget the impassable distances between humanity and divinity, did not become significant in art until the middle classes were able to call the tune.

During this period there was even a brief interlude of pure classical (not pseudo-classical!) art, such as Europe has not produced since, not even in the days of Goethe and Winckelmann. A number of reports, beginning as early as the twelfth century, show us that some men had begun to see the beauty of antique statuary from a point of view entirely new to north-west Europe. As in the case of Hildebert of Lavardin, among others, the first sparks of a genuine aesthetic enthusiasm for the works of antiquity were struck by archeological finds in their own lands and by acquaintance with the marvels of Rome itself. But although some slight, initial interest may have been stimulated by these finds, it was simply the idealism of the knightly culture which was taking shape. France led the way with the works in Chartres and Rheims, and Germany followed shortly afterwards with the statues of *Ecclesia* and *Synagoge*, the Angel on the Pillar of Judgement and the relief showing the death of Mary in Strassburg. In Bamberg the figures of *Synagoge*, *Mary* and *Elizabeth* (?), and the *Rider* provide further examples. They all show a high degree of feeling for idealized reality; the complete human being, ' beautiful and good ', emerges in a pure, monumental form, complete both physically and mentally.

Finally this period made one more important step towards a profane bias in the treatment of effigies on tombs. The earliest of these to survive is that of the anti-king Rudolf von Rhein-

---

[1] It was, admittedly, the new, anti-aristocratic approach which proclaimed itself in the ascetic sermons of sin and hell—in the style of Heinrich von Melk, for example —but this approach was still unable to exert any influence through art, because the patrons and protectors of artists were still, for the most part, secular or church nobles.

felden (d. 1080), in the Cathedral of Merseburg.   In the second half of the twelfth century these effigies on tombs became general.   It was as though persons enjoying a superior position in this life were attempting to leave something of their person and substance behind even after death!   Down to this time the mediaeval world, exclusively transcendental in its orientation, had disapproved of and even forbidden such ostentation, but it was powerless to control the new assessment of human character which inspired these effigies.   But as is to be seen so often in similar circumstances, there was no conscious attempt to make a clean break and eliminate traditional religious conceptions; the method rather was to modify the attitude of the church until a place for the new was found within it.   Thus, however incongruous the presence of grave-monuments in places of worship may seem, from the later Middle Ages onwards we find more and more churches erecting these signs of mortal aspirations to immortality.   Moreover, the figures show none of those external signs of decrepitude and decay which the preachers of repentance and asceticism loved so much; these dead men and women were offered to the eyes of those who should follow them in idealized, youthful beauty or in the full strength of manhood.[1] Of course, there was no intention to leave behind ' portraits ' of the dead; the sole intention was to ensure that posterity should be reminded of the rank and dignity of the deceased.   As early as the thirteenth century, however, artists had acquired a high degree of skill in depicting heads of decided character and personality, types which would reflect the rank and the activities of the deceased when alive.   To appreciate this, one need only look at the figures of the founders in Naumburg (about 1250), which, even if they are not real tomb-effigies in the true sense of the word, all aim to make good past neglect for these long departed souls, by securing from posterity the praise due to them.   They show an amazing variety of very earth-bound, individual characters (in itself evidence that the ideal, knightly type was no longer the sole model) including a few very un-holy ones!   And they stand

---

[1] Only the morbid mentality at the end of the Middle Ages developed a taste for tomb-effigies showing the resigned features, scored with pain and sorrow, of old men exhausted with the vagaries of this life.

around the high altar, the essential centre of worship in the house of God!

Only by such concessions could the church arrive at an honourable compromise with the layman's independence of spirit. In their own way these tomb-effigies had the same significance as the success of scholasticism in finding a place for secular learning within the ecclesiastical system. In both cases it was made to appear as though these new features were serving the church. But the pressure from within exerted by these individualistic and secular forces on the religious structure which housed them was steadily increased by their very presence there.[1]

---

[1] For the preceding, cf. W. Pinder, *Die Kunst der deutschen Kaiserzeit bis zum Ende der staufischen Klassik* (5th edn., Frankfurt, 1952); and W. Pinder, *Die Kunst der ersten Bürgerzeit* (3rd edn., Frankfurt, 1952)—to the middle of the fifteenth century.

CHAPTER IV

THE DECLINE

FROM THE END OF THE HOHENSTAUFEN PERIOD TO THE REFORMATION

GREAT progress had been made in all aspects of civilization, as well as in politics and religion, during the Hohenstaufen period. It was the most creative and, intellectually, the most important epoch of the Middle Ages; indeed it was one of the summits in the development of European culture. It was *then* and not at the time of the Renaissance, that what Burckhardt called 'the discovery of the world and man within it' really began. Even the first steps in this new outlook on life were on a grand and noble scale. Not until this time, for instance, had there been any expression of western European culture and thought in literary works of permanent value. In this respect the Renaissance and Humanism were both vastly inferior to the age of the Hohenstaufen.

All the themes which arose then were carried on into the ebbing Middle Ages. But it seems as though succeeding generations suffered under the wealth and complexity of their inheritance. The means with which they had been endowed brought with them demands and challenges which could no longer be met. It was not that the vitality of the Middle Ages was already exhausted. On the contrary, the period was possessed by a nervous disquiet which was liable to burst out into feverish activity; commerce, industry and the business of daily life were conducted with unflagging energy. It was the power to create, to press forward, that was lacking in the declining Middle Ages. People were unable to find a course or an objective among all the contradictory choices open to them; they could only unravel and dissect them further. As H. Heimpel has put it, the period 'marked time'; it was always on the move without getting any further. Not until the transition to the modern period did any new impulses arise to lead men out of this labyrinth of aims and purposes (see below, p. 111). And these new impulses signified the end of the Middle Ages.

DOUBT AND INDECISION

Life in the later Middle Ages was characterized in all its aspects by doubt and indecision. Let us first consider the political sphere. During the twelfth and thirteenth centuries definite steps had been taken towards the formation of national or territorial states in the 'modern' sense of the word. To a certain extent these steps had been successful, in so far as they had superseded the political implications of feudalism. But this development failed to fulfil its early promise; for the most part the territorial states regressed and decayed—naturally without any corresponding gain for the Empire, which was too far gone. What followed was merely an inextricable tangle of independent and pseudo-independent principalities, which crippled one another in interminable, senseless wars. The political scene in Germany, indeed throughout Europe, in the fourteenth and fifteenth centuries was little short of chaotic.[1]

It was the same in the social sphere. A new class, the middle class, had established a place for itself in the social structure, which up to then had consisted solely of peasants and aristocrats. The middle classes were determined to play as great a part as possible in social life, but they were unable to secure full privileges or leadership. The remainder of the Middle Ages must be regarded as a period of class struggles leading to the complete disintegration of the old structure of society. Even the individual classes were no longer distinct units, complete in themselves (examples of this will be given presently). In spite of the mutual hatred and contempt which they expressed so loudly and so often, they were full of covetous jealousy; each class saw the others as 'higher' or more profitable ranks in society. They would all have liked to change places, so, naturally, they remained just as they were.

Finally, there was the sphere of religion and ethics, concerned with the problem of the right way of life. Once more, even more violently than before, the two strongest forces of the time, secular

[1] Cf. G. Barraclough, *The Origins of Modern Germany* (Oxford, 1946), chap. 12.

society with all that it offered, and otherworldliness with its pious yearnings, its threats and admonitions, divided men's minds—especially middle-class minds. They could find no way of satisfying both and so were torn between the two extremes. One major factor contributing to this was the circumstance that industrious, but uncreative, imitators had desiccated knowledge and learning to a brittle, sterile intellectualism. The really urgent problems of philosophy were avoided. Theology moved along secluded paths away from the world in which men lived, and so was unable to give a lead in the burning questions of the day, in orientating the standards and forms of life. The only fields which did show some creative initiative were architecture and the pictorial arts. Even in these we can see evidence of the instability of character and the spiritual excesses of this decrepit age; but it cannot be denied that it was the wealth of fine art produced at this time that was responsible for the aureole with which the Romantics adorned the Middle Ages, and which still serves as a brilliant cover for so many shallow and sordid aspects of the period.

Sedlmayr's lament over the loss of the focal elements in human society—as reflected in art—is perhaps not as modern as it seems.[1] It is to be found in a poet writing in the period of knightly decline, Ulrich von Lichtenstein (d. about 1275). He resigned in despair from the knightly policy of ' pleasing both God and this world' and declared that whoever would possess all the things of this world at once must, by the same token, lose everything, for ' he lingers here and lingers there,/he has no centre, he has no end ' (*er sûmt sich hie und sûmt sich dort,/ern hat die mitte, ern hat daz ort.*) This is the signature of the Middle Ages in decline; there is no longer any ' centre ' or any ' end '. ' The period was united in its lack of unity; its style was a lack of style in everything, life, literature and thought. People could no longer direct their efforts; they had become uncertain of themselves. . . . For this new age was not yet strong enough to keep a grasp on the old nor to make the new succeed; they had not yet set their hearts sufficiently on the new age '.[2] However we look at the period it shows only a multitude of tangled, disfiguring lines.

[1] Hans Sedlmayr, *Art in Crisis: the Lost Centre* (London, 1957).
[2] W. Rehm, ' Kulturverfall und spätmittelhochdeutsche Didaktik ', ZPh XXV (1927), 329 sqq.

But we must not allow this to obscure the fact that, even in the late Middle Ages, most people belonging to the lower orders of society, about which we have so few sources of information, must still have lived healthy, balanced lives. This fact, however, does not alter the general tendencies and character of the period. In those classes which defined the intellectual outlook—and these really did extend well down the social scale—a loud and gaudy extremism was predominant, pointing to a deep-rooted uncertainty in intellectual and spiritual matters.

As the curtain came down on the Middle Ages, however, the scene changed. New forces and centres appeared; new nuclei took shape, which attracted the less vigorous elements and absorbed them in a 'process of natural selection'.[1] Such new formations then expanded until they in their turn affected every aspect of life.

In politics the 'Great Powers' on whom the balance of power in Europe was soon to be based, consolidated their positions afresh, whilst in Germany a limited number of relatively large territorial states secured all the political key-positions for themselves. In the development of the social classes the German middle class were pushed back into insignificance for another three hundred years—in fact, until the French Revolution; they ceased to be an active, decisive force in history. Similarly the lower nobility lost their political power. Although the peasantry had shown promise of becoming a considerable power in politics and society, they receded into passive anonymity after the terrible disaster of 1525. Thus the 'process of natural selection' decided entirely in favour of the ruling nobility, and of rapidly developing territorial absolutism; this is one of the most remarkable regressions in history. The new currents in philosophy, ethics and religion, however, were represented by the movements called Humanism, Reformation and Counter-Reformation; and through these, although only to a limited extent in the case of Humanism, society again found some sort of roots.

But the very existence of these new forces indicated that the Middle Ages were irrevocably played out. For even if genuinely mediaeval elements were incorporated in them, they were founded

[1] Heimpel, *Deutsches Mittelalter*, 112.

(with the partial exception of Humanism—however elastically this concept is defined) on premises which were directly opposed to the spirit of the Middle Ages. Hence they can be accepted without hesitation as the starting-point of a new epoch in history.[1]

SOCIAL CHANGE: TOWNS AND THE MIDDLE CLASSES

The outlook and the culture of the Middle Ages as outlined in the two preceding chapters was supported by a very narrow social basis. All our information for the early period is provided by higher church dignitaries and monks. After this the numbers of active participants in culture increased when secular knighthood came to make its contribution. But the ' people ', the ' masses ', remained dumb throughout the whole period. We know next to nothing about their thoughts and feelings, or how they coped with their lowly position and their bitterly hard life. As yet they were completely inarticulate in both material and intellectual matters. Moreover, these conditions were an essential feature of the cultural unity of the central Middle Ages, which was based on the fact that the masses (*vulgus*), by whose labour the church was maintained, were also the ' paving stones of the edifice of the church, over which (our) feet come and go ' (Honorius of Autun). But from the thirteenth century onwards, the greater mass of the people began to make themselves heard in Germany, and not long after this time they achieved a more important position than those classes which had hitherto been the sole agents of culture. These masses, however, were no longer organized in a hier-archical unity, composed of many steps and grades set one over the other (see above, p. 23); instead society had become a con-glomeration of highly diversified, friction-generating units.

The decisive feature was the new social unit, the town. Not only were economic and social activity in the towns subject to

---

[1] On the spirit of the period, cf. J. Huizinga, *The Waning of the Middle Ages* (1924); H. Pirenne, *La Fin du Moyen Age* (1931); H. Heimpel, ' Das deutsche Spätmittelalter, Charakter einer Zeit ', *Deutsches Mittelalter* (Leipzig, 1941), 105 sqq.; R. Stadelmann, *Vom Geist des ausgehenden Mittelalters . . . von Nikolaus Cusanus bis Sebastian Franck* (Heidelberg, 1929); W. Andreas, *Deutschland vor der Reformation, Eine Zeitwende* (5th edn., Stuttgart, 1948)—the most comprehensive account of the fifteenth century; H. Bechtel, *Wirtschaftsstil des deutschen Spätmittelalters . . . Wirtschaft, Gesellschafts-aufbau und Kunst von* 1350–1500 (Munich, 1930); J. W. Thompson, *Economic and Social History in the Later Middle Ages* (New York/London, 1931).

laws different from those obtaining in rural areas; the intellectual and spiritual outlook of the town-dweller were also entirely different. One aspect of the townsman was the book-keeping mentality of the commercial middle classes, which had a great influence on intellectual and religious matters (the ' Master Singers ' constitute one example and another will be given below on p. 140 sq.). The other aspect of the townsman was that he was much more versatile than his rural counterpart, who was tied to an agrarian economy. He had far more initiative, was more ' progressive ', but was inclined to be an easy target for propaganda and was therefore easily roused; he was easily influenced and exposed to the dangers of mass hypnotism. And in all these features the town reached out into the surrounding countryside. All in all the essential features of the Middle Ages in decline derived ultimately from the intellectual, economic and spiritual interests of the middle-class urban population.

In this sense, but only in this sense, we can say that the later Middle Ages were a bourgeois age. It would be quite wrong to suppose that Germany, along with the greater part of Europe, was already ' urbanized '. At least 75 per cent of the total population still lived on the land, and there were only twelve to fifteen German cities of ten to thirty thousand inhabitants. To these can be added twenty to thirty medium-sized towns of two to ten thousand inhabitants and several hundred small and minute towns, which were more like walled villages than towns in the modern sense. Economically the town had close connexions with the countryside about it; the majority of citizens were ' field tenants ' (*Ackerbürger*), having fields, meadows, vineyards, etc. outside the town gates and keeping the normal domestic animals of all sizes inside the town walls. Even as late as the fifteenth century in Germany all the livestock was collected each morning by the town herdsmen and driven out to the common pastures. The way of life, and consequently the mentality, of the lower ranks of citizens were very much like those of the rural population.

The population of medium and large towns was divided into two, and in the last century or so of the Middle Ages into three distinct classes or estates. First came the patrician class of wholesale merchants and financiers (the ' dynasties ', the ' honourables').

I

This class piled up wealth in sums which preceding generations could scarcely have imagined, by speculative enterprises which were as bold and far-sighted as they were socially and ethically unscrupulous. They were the operators of a completely uncontrolled economy, highly individualist and quite soon to become capitalist. After them came the artisan class, organized under the guild system and guided only by their prime objective of ensuring a solid, comfortable existence. This meant eliminating all risks and all competition; it was a system which regulated their lives down to the last detail and effectively smothered all initiative. Finally, there was a ' third estate ', a mass of dependent citizens without possessions, almost, if not completely, the equivalent of the modern proletariat. Especially towards the end of the Middle Ages the majority of journeymen, for whom the closed-shop policy of the guilds had made it impossible to become master, ended as members of this class. For the rest it comprised apprentices, day-labourers, workers in the domestic crafts (particularly the cloth industry), beggars and wasters of all kinds.

Obviously there were bitter and frequently violent fights for power between these social groups. At first it was the guilds challenging the patricians for a fair share in municipal government, but later the proletariat became more and more rebellious and asserted itself against these two proprietary classes. The social structure in the medium and large towns of Germany at the end of the Middle Ages was shockingly unhealthy and full of menace for the future. In many of them between one and two-fifths of the population owned nothing at all; in Augsburg, the centre of the cloth industry in southern Germany, this applied to two-thirds. There were towns—Ravensburg, for instance—where three-quarters of the total wealth was in the hands of only four-and-a-half per cent of the inhabitants; others—for example Erfurt and Fribourg in Switzerland—where more than half the total wealth was owned by a group of citizens representing only two per cent of the population.

The privileged legal position of the church, consequent upon development of the Gregorian programme, was a more widespread source of serious disturbance. Church possessions, representing about one-third of the total area of Germany, were exempt from all taxation. It was a deadweight burden on the national economy. The clergy were not answerable to secular law in any civil or criminal matters. Furthermore, clerical estates, because they had the equivalent of 'extra-territorial rights', were privileged competitors against the towns in industry and commerce. Both the towns and the territorial rulers were bitter, unrelenting enemies of this 'state within a state'; they tried to destroy, or at least to diminish, clerical privileges, in the hope of being able to use church lands to ease the burden of taxation. They also tried to bring the clergy under the same law as other subjects. Hatred of the clergy, which frequently flared up in violent risings, particularly in episcopal towns, was not the result of purely religious antipathies, but of economic and social conditions. It was because the clergy as a class claimed important rights and privileges even in secular matters.

As this account shows, in spite of the restraining effect of the theory upheld by the guilds that rank depended upon occupational status (see below p. 127), even in the towns there was to all intents and purposes an aristocratic form of government based on birth, power and wealth. And this was essentially a *static* form of government—a principle to which the Middle Ages remained faithful from beginning to end. Even the great popular preachers from the thirteenth to the fifteenth centuries, who condemned such a multitude of vices, and who always interceded on behalf of the weaker party, made no attempts to shake this principle. Recent research has left intact very little of the old, idealized picture which the Romantics drew of a just and Christian hierarchy of estates in the mediaeval town.

The ideal did not exist even within the guilds. They probably did care for the social interests of their members, but there are scarcely any traces of attempts at co-operation between the different classes and trade-groups. The guilds also thought on oligarchic lines as far as they were able. The farmers on the land belonging to the towns had to accept dictated prices; no man who was not a citizen was allowed to practise a trade within the 'forbidden mile' radius of the town; the servitude of peasants under town or guild rule was just as degrading as the position of their fellows under feudal, territorial lords. For a few genera-

tions the guilds probably did, on the whole, fulfil their social
obligations to the community of the town, but in time they
became even more rigidly insulated in their caste-spirit and the
selfish interests of individual groups. This gave rise to the
problem of the permanent journeymen. The most widely distributed reform pamphlet of the fifteenth century, the *Reformatio
Sigismundi* (about 1430–1440), strongly denounces economic
cliques, the self-seeking of the guilds and their dishonest intrigues
in the town councils. It demands that the guilds be abolished in
the interest of the common good and replaced by free trade and
manufacture, in which ' every man shall be like the next ' (*ider-
mann dem andern geleich*).

Both in their sermons and in their tracts the popular preachers
were most severe against avarice, usury and the exploitation of
the weaker party. These were the most outstanding evils of the
time. People simply could not maintain their ethical principles
in the face of the great opportunities to gain profit and own
property, which had been brought about by the revival of a money
economy. In effect Christian morals were entirely lacking,
particularly in so far as justice and the obligations of rulers to
their subjects, and of the privileged to the dispossessed, were
concerned. Naturally this was most aggravated in cases where
the possibilities of securing wealth and power were most blatant.
The prohibition of the taking of interest by the church, which
simply identified interest with usury, became a mere façade. It
may from time to time have caused a few twinges of conscience,
in spite of the petty casuistries invented to get round it in a
' legitimate ' way; but it no longer had the power to influence
business as a whole. It was, in fact, no longer applicable to the
new conditions. Even the church, which had once so strongly
insisted on the prohibition of dealings in money, exploited the
new, capitalistic type of economy, and nowhere more actively
than in the papal curia. For a long time neither the public sense
of moral responsibility nor any form of social legislation by the
state could keep pace with developments. The most effective
social measure was the ecclesiastical institution of almsgiving and
charitable foundations for the poor and the sick. There can be
no doubt that these did alleviate the most pressing evils, but they

did not affect the source of these evils; the real essence of the problem was left untouched. So many of these fine, charitable foundations, such as the almshouses established by the Fuggers in Augsburg, were the outcome of an economic policy based on pure coercion. Others were prompted by troubled consciences activated by approaching death. The need for some kind of atonement—for the salvation of their souls—was interpreted in a more concrete and literal form by these business tycoons and their contemporaries than had been the case with the numerous donors to the church in the earlier Middle Ages.

Middle-class society in the late Middle Ages was extremely pious (see below p. 137). But the other-worldly, Christian super-structure to life, to which it still clung so stubbornly, was no longer supported in social life. There was no real relationship between the two. The demands of the new way of life were too unrelenting, and the standards of traditional Christian morals could not be adjusted to meet them.

The rise of the middle classes brought a very impressive reserve of national strength to the top. Their achievements in the most varied fields prove that they were far from being diseased and decadent. But their rather brutal and erratic vitality could not easily be directed into suitable channels. To find out and establish such channels should have been their first concern. This is most obvious in their political activities. The towns threw away their finest opportunities by adopting a blinkered, parochial policy, based on mutual mistrust and jealousy. The traditional religious element was still strong in the middle classes; but they were easily led into contradiction with it, and the result was a dangerous split in the character of the class as a whole.[1]

---

[1] On developments in the towns, cf. Fr. Rörig, *Die europäische Stadt* (Propyläen-weltgeschichte Vol. IV) (Berlin, 1932); H. Pirenne, *Medieval Cities, Their Origins and the Revival of Trade* (4th edn., 1946); E. Ennen, *Frühgeschichte der europäische Stadt* (1953); J. Strieder, *Werden und Wachsen des europäischen Frühkapitalismus* (Propyläen-weltgeschichte Vol. IV); A. Störmann, *Die städtischen Gravamina gegen den Klerus* (Munich, 1916); G. Caro, *Sozial und Wirtschaftsgeschichte der Juden im Mittelalter und in der Neuzeit* (2 vols., Leipzig, 1908, 1920); L. Finkelstein, *Jewish Self-Government in the Middle Ages* (New York, 1925).

THE NOBILITY IN THE LATE MIDDLE AGES

All the developments of the period which reflect to the credit of the middle class automatically argue against the previous ruling class, the nobility. The period of greatness of the knighthood as a class came to an end about the middle of the thirteenth century; after this date there was no remedy for its decline. But although there were unmistakable signs of decadence in the knightly life of the late Middle Ages, as a class it continued to be a considerable force.

The knighthood found a number of ways of averting the economic crisis threatening them. The most primitive, and the most destructive, was the profession of arms. With complete disdain for all ethical considerations knights sold themselves by the thousand as mercenaries to the highest bidder, whatever his nationality. At home they adopted the equally despicable calling of robber baron or simple highwayman. There were still some knights who wandered aimlessly over the face of the earth in search of adventure; but they had little in common with the nobly questing knights of the great court epics. One of them, Oswald von Wolkenstein (d. 1445), has left us a frank picture of his contemporaries which is full of bitter self-irony.

Another way out was to enter the church; the more lucrative positions (particularly in cathedral chapters) were monopolized by the nobility. The younger sons of knights found an ever open asylum in the church, whatever their personal preferences or talents.[1] But the more serious and industrious knights found positive ways of adapting themselves to the new epoch. Many studied law to prepare for a position, as *milites literati*, at the courts or in the administrative offices of the territorial rulers. But in Germany at least, they never quite attained the same standards or reputation in these fields as their colleagues of middle-class origin. Many merged into the middle-class upper layer of urban society and joined in trading enterprises whilst retaining possession of their rural estates. There were frequent marriages between knights and the daughters of rich merchant princes.

---

[1] Cf. A. Schulte, *Der Adel und die deutsche Kirche im Mittelalter* (Stuttgart, 1910); G. G. Coulton, *Five Centuries of Religion*, Vol. IV (1950), 328 sqq. (' Younger children are cast into religion as we cast the worse puppies into the water '); G. Barraclough, *Papal Provisions* (Oxford 1935), 38 sqq., 54 sqq.

Many members of the knighthood were very critical of this at first, but it was soon admitted that it was befitting to their rank. Other knights were not too proud to descend from their castled crags and perform menial tasks in their own fields. This type of knight soon degenerated far towards a peasant way of life— ' many a nobleman would rather load a full sack of corn on to his cart than wield a lance at a joust '—but they kept out of debt and were not destructive.

It is a colourful picture and full of contradictions. The scale extends from complete identification with the industrious middle classes to useless dissipation; from effeminate court lap-dogs, with dyed and waved hair (as described, for instance, by the chronicler Thomas Eberndorffer in the middle of the fifteenth century) to coarse, brawling sots. But they did not relinquish their class-consciousness; indeed, it even became more rigid and arrogant. Hereditary knighthood became more important than knighthood conferred for personal services. Peter von Andlau wrote in the middle of the fifteenth century: ' Even if they come from the most poverty-stricken estate in the country or in the mountains, or, more accurately, from a wolf's lair, they still consider themselves real noblemen, and have no use for wisdom, virtue and other such things. . . .' One is immediately reminded of Hutten's mordant description of a knightly castle in his famous letter to Willibald Pirckheimer. And how aggressively they proclaimed their class-consciousness! Among the seven special attributes which befit a knight the ' Code of Knighthood ' (*Ritter-spiegel*) of Johannes Rothe (d. 1439) lists: a golden ring with a precious stone for his finger; an obedient squire to carry his sword, so that he is not obliged to carry it himself and look like an executioner; the right to wear a multi-coloured surcoat; and the privilege of having water poured over his hands and being given a clean towel after meals. Little wonder, then, that Seifried Helbling (about 1300), well disposed though he was towards the class as a whole, should sigh: ' Then I thought to myself, remember now Sir Parzival; how *he* strove to find the Grail and to be an honourable knight! '

Nevertheless the high ideals of the past remained alive in memory, and there began a remarkable revival within the knighthood from the mid-fourteenth century onwards. It was at this time that the numerous orders of knighthood were instituted, mostly centred on particular princely courts, frequently with odd, droll names. There were the orders of ' The Brooch ', and ' The Griffon ', ' The Unicorn ', ' The Lock of Hair '; in Burgundy there was the ' Order of the Golden Fleece ', and in England ' The Order of the Garter '. Perhaps the most serious of all were the ' Narren vom guten Ton ' (The Order of the Fools of Good Manners) which started on the Lower Rhine about 1380. They all aimed at fostering a truly knightly way of life in their members, of making them aware of their ethical obligations and the religious aspects of the knightly code. They also tried to check the tendency to relegate women to the status of mere instruments of sexual gratification, as they are represented in the most popular non-religious book of the Middle Ages, the *Roman de la Rose* and in many contemporary short stories. There is no doubt that these circles were inspired by the best of intentions to raise a rather brutal society, completely possessed by the most primitive instincts, to a higher, nobler, code of behaviour; but they soon took refuge in a world of glittering deceptions, in a great ' social game ', as Huizinga put it. It was rather a dream-pageant of what was good and noble, ruled by minutely pre-scribed ceremonial procedure. But there was no reality of knightly life behind it, because the real thing was no longer possible.

THE PEASANTRY IN THE LATE MIDDLE AGES

The other old social class, the peasantry, rose in open revolt against the established order at the end of the Middle Ages. The economic and social reasons for this rising seem to lie in the increasingly severe oppression of the peasants by the manorial lords and the new princely administrations which developed in the course of the fifteenth century. This was a retrogression, for after the thirteenth century the peasants' conditions in most parts of Germany had been by no means hopeless or discouraging. For a number of reasons the value of peasant labour and agri-cultural produce had risen and this had led to the substitution of a contractual for a purely servile relationship between peasant and lord. Farmers, organized in village communities, gained a certain amount of independence. However limited this may have been, it did produce a class-consciousness among them which steadily increased. Modest comfort, in some cases relative wealth, enabled them to maintain appropriate outward appearances, which turned the heads of many. They acquired ambitions above their rank and strutted about like their masters, boastful and pretentious, in knightly armour and showy dress. Nobles degenerated into peasants, peasants degenerated into knights. In both cases they aped only the baser side of their models. The process is described very realistically in the poem *Meier Helmbrecht* (about 1250). It ends with the horrible death of a peasant outlaw, who had become the scourge and oppressor of his own class.

No class was so ill spoken of as the peasantry in the late Middle Ages. Contemporary literature directed every imaginable form of ridicule, hatred and vulgar abuse at these ' boors ', ' coarse felt-hats ', ' clod-hoppers ', etc. Neidhart von Reuenthal (d. before 1250) started it with satire that was realistic but as yet harmless. His example was followed by a number of vulgar, malicious ' pseudo-Neidharts ' in the fourteenth and fifteenth centuries. In the festival plays of the towns, written by and for the middle classes, the peasants took the stage as Harry Dung, Fred Winegullet, Harry Wheygobbler, Stinknose, Dripnose, etc. Nothing is bad enough for the peasants: *Rustica gens optima flens pessima gaudens*. A canon of Zurich, Felix Hemmerlein (d. 1458), prescribed as a recipe against peasant arrogance that they should have their houses and farms burned down every fifty years— the reference being to the Old Testament ' Jubilee Year '. Among the precepts for noblemen composed at the end of the fifteenth century appear resolutions such as: ' We'll burn it down about their ears and singe them like fat sows . . . before we slit their throats '.

Some voices, however, were raised in protest against the brutal tyranny of the lords. It could not be denied that everybody lived on the peasants' toil in blazing sun and bitter cold. Konrad von Amenhusen's *Book of Chess* (1337) warns that the pawn (i.e. the peasant) can take any piece on the board and may even checkmate the king.

The peasant benefited also from the brave intercession of the popular preachers on behalf of the suppressed classes of society. This implied a totally new approach. Throughout the Middle Ages the lords of the feudal hierarchy had sheltered behind religion, claiming that the established order was the work of God, and must therefore be accepted without question. Even Thomas Aquinas, who was always strongly attached to the Aristotelian law of nature, could think of no alternative to some men being *sui iuris* and others *iuris alterius*—i.e. free and unfree. But now the will of God was made to demand the opposite! God had made all men equal. This principle was formulated during the Peasants' Revolt in England in 1381 in the well-known verse: ' When Adam delved and Eve span, who was then the gentleman? ' In support of this Christian interpretation of natural law it was pointed out that Christ had come to serve *all* men. It was intolerable that one man could say to another, ' You are mine to dispose of'; for Christ redeemed *all* men by His wounds and His martyrdom, ' so that no man shall be elevated above the other, for we all share the same redemption and the same freedom, whether of noble or common birth . . . ' (*Reformatio Sigismundi*). A Doctor Seitz of Württemberg, writing towards the end of the fifteenth century, said: ' He gave birth to all of us equally, and Christ paid the same price for each and all of us '. Hence the standard adopted by the peasants during the revolt of 1525 bore a kneeling peasant looking up to a picture of the Saviour on the cross, above which was the device ' Nothing but the justice of God '.

Indeed, contemporary prophecies of an imminent millenium (see below, p. 143) placed their hopes in the peasants, declaring them to be the true, chosen people of God. As early as 1352 Rulman Merswin wrote, ' Then shall come to pass great miracles by the peasants '. And the *Reformatio Sigismundi* says: ' The treasure of righteousness is perhaps reserved for the more humble of men (both in town and country) '.

Such was the cry of the revolutionaries—in the name of the same commandment of God and the same Christian message as that which the whole of the preceding Middle Ages had invoked to support the old social order. The practical and ideological success of the revolution was negligible, but it was the first real attack against almost a thousand years of tradition, and it is a significant indication of the way in which the period was preparing its own end.[1]

Social and Religious Confusion

All ranks of society alike were disturbed by recurrent social crises throughout the period. This background must be kept in mind whenever the structure of mediaeval society is discussed. The middle classes were the most active intellectually but, in spite of this, and in spite of their vigour in winning a place in the sun, they were never able to produce a coherent conception of their place as a class in the social order, such as the knights had evolved as a matter of course almost as soon as they were recognizable as a class. For that they were too divided within themselves. They were never able to shake off the traditional idea that there were only three classes; nobles, peasants and priests. Freidank said that these three were created by God but that men of commerce were 'created by the devil's wiles' (*geschuf des tiuvels list*). With all their activity in literature they never give us a pattern of their real selves. We have no clear picture of their ambitions or the basic considerations which controlled their lives. Neither the distinguished, urban patricians nor the honest, comfortable master-craftsmen had heroes in their own image to serve as models of behaviour, such as the nobility had once had in Erec and Iwein, Parzival and Willehalm. At the very most a burger could look to *The Good Gerhard* by Rudolf von Ems (1220–50), and even in this case the author was of noble descent.

Thus, at a time when life was progressing more strongly and quickly than ever before, men's minds were turned to the past. The middle classes saw the passing of the 'good old days' as the

---

[1] On the peasantry, cf. G. G. Coulton, *The Medieval Village* (1925); G. v. Below, *Geschichte der deutschen Landwirtschaft des Mittelalters*, hg. v. Friedrich Lütge (Jena, 1937); K. S. Bader, 'Bauernrecht und Bauernfreiheit im späteren Mittelalter', HJb, LXI (1941), 51 sqq.; G. Franz, *Der deutsche Bauernkrieg*, 2 vols. (Munich ,1933, 1935), Fr. v. Bezold, 'Die "armen Leute" und die deutsche Literatur des späteren Mittelalters', *Aus Mittelalter und Renaissance* (Munich, 1918); E. G. Gudde, *Social Conflicts in Medieval German Poetry* (Berkeley, 1934); R. Radbruch, *Der deutsche Bauernstand zwischen Mittelalter und Neuzeit* (Munich, 1941)—the peasant in the art of the period.

prime weakness of their own age; and they did their best to imitate the forms and standards of the nobility as a class. The greatest ambitions of a man of the upper middle classes were to take part in tourneys, to have a coat of arms and a family tree, and to own a feudal estate and patents of nobility. By this time it was possible to buy the latter—at a price! Stories of knightly chivalry, in the courtly manner, were always extremely popular with middle-class writers and their public. In spite of the self-confidence which wealth and power had brought them ('wealthy worthiness' as Rudolf von Ems put it) noble rank was still the criterion of this middle-class society.

Times were bad—but the immense output of didactic literature was trying to improve things. Some of the authors, such as Hugo von Montfort (d. 1423) and his contemporary Hans Vintler, were of noble birth, but the majority came from the middle classes. Hugo von Trimberg was the author of a very popular moralizing poem, the *Renner* (about 1300), of more than twenty-four thousand lines, in which sin, repentance and atonement are continually brought together. Other noteworthy names, among a great many more, are Heinrich Frauenlob (d. 1338), Teichner (d. 1377), Peter Suchenwirt (about the same time), Muskatblüt and Hans Rosenblüt (both in the first half of the fifteenth century). With the possible exceptions of Teichner and von Trimberg's *Renner*, they all subscribe more or less to knightly ethical ideals.

There had been a kind of didactic poetry in the heyday of knighthood (Freidank, Thomasin von Zirclaria, Windsbeke), but it had only supplemented the ideals expressed in more elevated literary form in the court epics. In these epics men had found relief by confessing what was weighing on their minds, namely, how a (knightly) human being, existing in this world, could integrate and balance his own personality. But the new middle-class didacticism offered to the reader neither living experience nor genuine ideals; as the word indicates, it was nothing more than theoretical instruction, scolding like a schoolmaster and moralizing like a bigot.

This new didacticism had neither the strength nor the courage to insist on the severe demands which the ideal of an integrated personality would have imposed. It was completely negative. The change in the character of didactic writing can be observed even before the middle of the thirteenth century, in the *Warning* (i.e. the warning of death) and the second part of Windsbeke. It was a reversion to a primitive ' black and white ' formulation of a crudely dualistic morality, and this morality was, in fact, completely materialistic. It gives the impression that people were able to see only the ugliness, meanness, vice and degeneracy of society—and the gruesome retribution waiting in the world beyond. Heinrich von Neustadt, writing shortly after 1300, made the soul revile the body, as the cause of its external misery, as follows: 'O, wicked flesh, fodder of worms,/belly of decay and barrel of stinks ' (*O boses fleisch, du maden az,/du fuler buch, du stankes vaz*). In the same context another poem says: ' Cursed be the day and the night which brought us two (i.e. body and soul) together ' (*verflucht sy nacht und tag,/do ich zu dir ie wart gesant*).[1] Man is only ' weak dung and despicable ashes ', declared Suchenwirth (who was a great admirer of the knighthood!), and Vintler, of noble birth, quotes Innocent III (see above, p. 69) extensively in his reviling on the infamy of all that is human. It was impossible to exaggerate the evidence of the devil at work all around one. This provided most fertile ground for the contemporary belief in witches; it was a general conviction of the times that ' all the visible happenings of this world can be the work of demons '. In *The Devil's Net* (about 1415) the snares of the devil are minutely described in more than thirteen thousand lines. Suchenwirth and Muskatblüt both wrote long, moralizing allegories on the subject of the seven deadly sins. The results of such efforts are summed up by Heinrich der Teichner in the following lines: ' Hence my conscience bids me flee/from all the works of this earth;/whoever is able to see through this life/will curse it worse than a mangy dog. . . . No man is so complete in virtue/that he can escape from it without stain/if he has anything at all to do

---

[1] Compare this with a sentence from Thomas Aquinas: 'A soul united with the body is more like God than one parted from the body, for then it possesses more completely its own true nature'. This is a striking example, which shows how misleading it would be to base accounts of ' the mediaeval outlook on life ' on Scholasticism alone. Even this Thomism was virtually restricted to the Dominicans for a very long time.

with it . . . ' (*so heizt mich min gewissen vliehen/all daz werltlich ist getan;/swer die werlt ahten kunt,/der flüch sie wirs dan einen hund . . . . Ez ist niemant so tugent vol, /der von ir kom ane meil,/gewint er an ir deheinen teil . . . .*).

Their concept of what is ' moral ' seems to have been formed under the spell of sin, death and hell; goodness is perceived and explained entirely from an initial assumption of evil. Usually they got no farther than a discussion of evil and its consequences.

Such was the mentality behind the nervous tension typical of the late Middle Ages. It found relief in demonstrations of mass hysteria and the enjoyment of gruesome horrors. The Flagellants were ecstatic in their obsession with the terrors of sin and hell; they began in Italy about 1260 and became particularly strong in Germany as a consequence of the Black Death of 1348–9. There were fearful representations in both literature and art of the savage creatures of the devil, who were said to brawl with the angels around death-beds for possession of the victim's soul. For the benefit of the uneducated this theme was enlarged upon in a new type of popular literature, a kind of *ars moriendi*. In the middle of the fourteenth century the theme of the Dance of Death was developed in art and literature. Charnel-houses, piled high with bones, were erected in the graveyards (see below, p. 143).

Even the popular preachers, such as Berthold of Regensburg (d. 1272), John of Capestrano (d. 1456), an Italian who acquired a great following in Germany, Geiler von Kaysersberg (d. 1510), and many more who dominated the opinions of the masses at that time, preferred to keep to the same old ponderous sermons on sin, repentance and punishment or to terrify their audiences with long-winded rantings about death and hell. Capestrano, for instance, once flourished a skull from the pulpit, saying: ' Look, and see what remains of all that once pleased you, or that which once led you to sin. The worms have eaten it all '. People were most susceptible to such cheap effects in those days; influenced by a sermon of this kind a hundred and twenty members of the University of Leipzig entered monasteries simultaneously.[1]

[1] For the preceding, cf. W. Stammler, *Von der Mystik zum Barock* (1400–1600).

Nevertheless, these popular preachers were much more tolerant and realistic than the theorizing didactics, who were mostly laymen. The preachers were too intimately acquainted with the masses, and had too much genuine sympathy for them, to refrain from pointing out some positive ways to happiness and salvation. Later Luther was to preach with rather presumptuous self-confidence, that the church had never recognized practical, secular pursuits; but this was incorrect. The contrary is demonstrated by the numerous ' addresses to the professions ' in the sermon literature of the Middle Ages, which warn and admonish the members of various callings about their professional duties. Some attempts were made to establish a Christian code of professional ethics; ' every Christian shall bear in mind, in what the office consists, to which he has been appointed by God ' (Tauler). ' The worldly pursuits of laymen, by which their mortal life is sustained, that they may praise and honour God ' are no less necessary than the work of monks and clerics, declared the Dominican Berthold Huenlein at the beginning of the fourteenth century. And Johannes Herolt, a Dominican, who died about 1468, said that the estate of matrimony was superior to other estates, because it was instituted by God Himself.

But the same Tauler regarded the secular estate as the lowest step to perfection, and said that the vocation of the evangelical councils (i.e. life in a cloister) was ' Much higher and quite different '. Against the favourable opinion on marriage, quoted above, there was a lot of coarse invective against women and family life, e.g. in the widely known *Consolatio Theologiae* by the Dominican Johann von Dambach (d. 1372) or in the malicious *Alphabet of Women* by Archbishop Antonino of Florence (d. 1459). We must not look for a constant line in all this, for there is none to be found. One can only look for a preponderance on one

(2nd edn., Stuttgart, 1950); A. Taylor, *Problems in German Literary History of the Fifteenth and Sixteenth Centuries* (New York, 1939); W. Rehm, ' Kulturverfall und spätmittelhochdeutsche Didaktik ', ZPh XXV (1927), 289 sqq.; A. Keller, *Fastnachtsspiele aus dem 15. Jahrhundert*, (Stuttgarter Literarischer Verein, Vols. 28–30 and 46), (Stuttgart, 1853–); W. French, *Medieval Civilization illustrated by the Fastnachtsspiele of Hans Sachs* (Göttingen, 1925); A. Hübner, *Die deutschen Geisslerlieder* (Berlin/Leipzig, 1931); W. Rehm, *Der Todesgedanke in der deutschen Dichtung vom Mittelalter bis zur Romantik* (Heidelberg, 1928); L. P. Kurtz, *The Dance of Death and the Macabre Spirit in European Literature* (New York, 1934); H. Stegemeier, *The Dance of Death in Folk Song, with an Introduction into the History of the Dance of Death* (Chicago, 1939).

side or the other—and it is obvious that the main bias was against worldly life and society, its values and material attributes.

The ideals associated with a Christian life had been defined exclusively by clerics, most of them monks, and it was their spiritual and emotional attitudes, purveyed by this edifying, popular literature, which penetrated into all ranks of society. They established the norms which laymen of all ranks had to accept. The well-known theory of a graded hierarchy of estates in the Middle Ages, according to which the functions necessary to Christian society as a whole were shared out impartially between clerks and laymen, who were considered to be complementary to one another, is not without its grain of truth. But the dominant, instinctive reaction of clerics and laymen alike, and particularly in periods of high religious tension, was to choose ' renunciation of the world ' as the truly Christian way of life. This lay behind Luther's decision to enter a monastery. But in the majority of cases renunciation was not seriously intended and was in fact impossible to attain. This may be perceived behind the strained proclamations of their ' worldly piety ' by the Humanists (see below, p. 163). The Middle Ages never succeeded in shedding the narrow, ascetic dress in which they had made their début. They clung to it even after historical development had left it far behind. The uncertain, vacillating attitude of the middle classes in the late Middle Ages shows this.

For life cannot be made to stand still. Even the didactic poets, while raising their moving complaints about the wickedness of the world, were mostly very appreciative of its more pleasant aspects; and quite often their fierce hostility towards ' base matter ' (*snoede materjen*, as Vintler put it) is not much in evidence in their conduct. The prophet raising a stiff forefinger in condemnation of this world and the easygoing hedonist were close neighbours. Both were allowed to go their own ways. Immediately after his lament over the loss of ' centre and end ' (see above, p. 110), Ulrich von Lichtenstein himself admits that ' The same delusion (of being able to serve both God and the world together) still deceives me/and really makes a fool of me ' (*derselbe wan mich triuget noch/und ich bin da mit geeffet doch*). Men worried continually about the discrepancy between what the world was really like and what it should be in theory. This was quite natural; but consciously or unconsciously they regarded it as something unavoidable.

About this time popular, middle-class literature split up into a number of distinct genres: folk-songs, fables, farces, festival plays, etc. They all contain much evidence of the vivid confusion and the full-blooded naturalism of contemporary life among the lower classes, both in town and country. In some of them we can hear pure and beautiful echoes of simple souls and enjoy their healthy, uninhibited originality; e.g. the song ' I heard a little sickle swishing ' (*Ich hört' ein Sichlein rauschen*). The natural joys of the senses were not neglected in this poetry. But even in such works there is an undercurrent of brutal coarseness, leering obscenity and crapulence. It seems as though nature was bent on revenge for all the abuse she had suffered at the hands of mediaeval theorists and was trying to wash all that was cheap and common up to the surface of human character from the depths to which it had been relegated. This generation was avid for all that the world had to offer (and it now had infinitely more to offer than in previous centuries), but at the same time it was aware of being restricted and constrained by its Christian conscience. They could find neither direction, proportion nor foundations for a really satisfactory, complete life, and so were easily led off into extremes of bad taste and poor style.[1]

The crass anomalies in thought and feeling in literature are accurate indications of the actual confusion of late mediaeval life. It was an age of intense religious life (see below, p. 137); all classes and ranks subscribed to found and maintain a profusion of charitable institutions; people were caught up in waves of self-sacrifice for great communal projects, such as the great city churches, which depended on religious inspiration as well as civic pride. Nevertheless, there is something quite horrifying about the general human and moral tone of the late Middle

[1] For the preceding paragraphs, cf. N. Paulus, ' Die Wertung der weltlichen Berufe im Mittelalter ', HJb. XXXII (1911), 725 sqq.; H. Denifle, *Luther und Luthertum* (2nd edn., Mainz, 1904), 133 sqq. (abundant material but convincing only in parts); A. Auer, *Johann von Dambach und die Trostbücher vom 11.–16. Jahrhundert* (Münster, 1928); H. Finke, *Die Frau im Mittelalter* (Kempten/Munich, 1912); L. Hess, *Die deutschen Frauenberufe des Mittelalters* (Munich, 1940).

K

Ages; and both high and low, church and lay, were equally responsible for it.

In all fields of political activity the Middle Ages had no need to wait for the precepts of Machiavelli justifying cold-blooded consideration of personal advantage at all costs. After the Empire had ceased to count for anything, little attention was paid to *pax et justitia* as the guiding lines of Christian politics. War was waged with the most brutal and cruel means available; e.g. the systematic burning and laying waste of undefended farm-lands. It was a generation which could hate and revile as scarcely any other period in history. And it would be difficult to devise a system of justice which made use of more frightful sadistic inventions for torturing and martyring. Most significant of all, these were carried out as public entertainment, which agitated the most brutal instincts of the masses. Ruthlessness in commercial affairs and the radical decline of business ethics among the urban middle classes have been mentioned above (p. 115). There was also complete freedom in sexual matters. Even smaller towns had their brothels, whose inmates enjoyed a place in local society; they were present at the official receptions of royalty and had their own pews in church. Most of these less creditable features of society had existed in previous centuries, but in the later Middle Ages they were visibly accentuated. It was no longer a case of isolated (even if rather frequent) human shortcomings and mistakes such as may be encountered in any society; on the contrary such things were a part of the average way of life, and can be said to define the spirit and character of the late Middle Ages.

Was there then, any such thing as a ' Christian ' culture of the late Middle Ages? Much points to an affirmative answer—above all, that the period wanted to be Christian. On the other hand a large part of the evidence points in a contrary direction, and so the query is justified. As a period it was not *worse* than others; but it had become less inhibited and less consistent in its collective motives and passions. This was because the standards and relationships of the old order had been whittled down without being succeeded by any effective substitutes. So people expended their efforts in all directions, in a ' facility of emotions, of tears and spiritual upheavals ',[1] which gives this period a unique character in the history of western culture.[2] People were completely at the mercy of their emotions. From there they drew the strength, to which we must credit their great artistic achievements, and at the same time their weakness. For in spite of all its robust vitality, society had to pay for this immoderate drain on its strength from within with a growing spiritual debility which more settled societies at other times have largely avoided.[3]

THE CHURCH IN THE LATE MIDDLE AGES

The crisis of the late Middle Ages reveals itself most clearly in the religious temper of the period and the different ways in which people expressed their piety. To make this clear we must go into the general situation of the church in the late Middle Ages. As is well known, the church at this time was decaying from within more seriously than ever before or since in its history. Pope Eugene IV (1421–47) once applied the words of Isaiah i, 6 to it: ' From the sole of the foot even unto the head there is no soundness in it '. The fact that ' bad ', ' unworthy ' popes, cardinals and bishops were so numerous compared with the conscientious, pious and upright men who were to be found in all ranks of the church, is not the decisive factor. On the contrary it was only a consequence of the fact that the Gregorian programme of power and domination had twisted the structure of the church as a whole. As early as the twelfth century Gerho von Reichersberg (d. 1169) was very much perturbed because the *ecclesia Romana* had turned into a *curia Romana*. He meant that the church was no longer primarily concerned with religion; it no longer represented the concept of the living *body of Christ*, but had been so distorted that both the church hierarchy and the

[1] Huizinga, *The Waning of the Middle Ages*, 14.

[2] Rilke's sonnet, *Gott im Mittelalter*, describes perfectly the spiritual outlook of the mediaeval middle classes, which was always in danger of a religious short-circuit.

[3] Cf. J. Schäfer, *Die kirchlichen, sittlichen und sozialen Zustände des 15. Jahrhunderts nach Dionysius Carthusiensis* (Tübingen, 1904); J. Löhr, *Methodisch-Kritische Beiträge zur Geschichte der Sittlichkeit des Klerus, besonders der Erzdiözese Köln, am Ausgang des Mittelalters* (Münster, 1910); P. Browe, *Beiträge zur Sexualethik des Mittelalters* (Breslau, 1932). For works on the history of individual towns and territories, see W. Andreas, *op. cit.*, 656.

congregation of the faithful had come to regard it rather as an earthly ' perfect society ', an administrative and juridical institution, and a state-like political power. The basic ailment of the church in the late Middle Ages was its willingness to allow its juridical functions to undermine its original religious purpose. Excommunication—banishment from the community of believers in Christ—was a religious disciplinary measure; but it was debased into the normal weapon against all kinds of political opposition. Eventually it came to be used against poor people whose taxes were overdue! Through the interdict the faithful of whole territories or countries were made to suffer the severest of religious penalties on account of a few people who may have been guilty or perhaps merely wrongly accused; or alternatively they were driven to look for spiritual consolation outside the church. The Inquisition, with its tortures, forced confessions, and executions—still sternly condemned as un-Christian by Bernard of Clairvaux—is a horrible piece of evidence of the extent to which Roman *public* law had prevailed over the principles of the church. The Roman curia was intensively centralized to control directly every aspect of the church. It claimed the right to make all church appointments, high and low, in all countries. It had the right to pass judgement in all legal disputes between members of the church. And its system of privileges and dispensations offered relief from all ecclesiastical requirements and regulations, even the most firmly established. No one had need to fear that the duty of priests to reside within their own parishes would be enforced, or that the canons against accumulating livings or electing immature boys to bishoprics would be applied. As a result all the most important concerns of the church came under the control of a bureaucracy organized like a business concern. This was all the more harmful because obviously no official system, however carefully developed and controlled, could hope to deal justly and competently with such an immense range of problems.

The main purpose behind the intensive centralization of the curia was to bring in money. Among the malignant growths in the body of the church this preoccupation with fiscal matters was hardly less insidious than its over-centralization. In those days the papal treasury employed the most thorough and expert system of taxation in Europe. All judgements and decisions of the church were to be had for money—and only for money. Judgement was given to the highest bidder at all levels of church officialdom. Payments for indulgences lined the coffers, not only of the pope, but also of many bishops and even of secular lords. Naturally, the example of the Roman curia was followed step by step down to the lowest ranks of the ecclesiastical hierarchy. The bishops increased their incomes without scruple, according to their opportunities and talents, through such expedients as payments for installation in livings, visitations and tacit permission for priests to keep concubines at the price of fixed conscience-money; parsons and priests exacted fees for every service apart from conducting public worship.[1]

Even holy things were automatically drawn into this system and assessed according to their earning power. And this was not merely due to individual abuse; it was openly and officially sanctioned by the church. Thus it is pointless to argue whether this or that pope or bishop was responsible since, from the time of its development in the thirteenth century, the system enveloped the whole body of the church so completely that no single pope, even with the best of intentions, could have checked it. There was continual talk of 'reform in head and members', but nothing came of it, for all the leading elements in society, including the territorial rulers, were irrevocably committed to the existing system. Even the most refined and far-seeing thinker of the whole period, Nicholas of Cues (see below, p. 148 sqq.), was not immune from it. He went about his rather shady dealings in livings without the slightest compunction, and was as stubborn as any, in his disputes at Brixen with Archduke Sigismund of

---

[1] For conditions at the papal curia and in the church, cf. J. Haller, *Papsttum und Kirchenreform* (Berlin, 1903); W. von Hofmann, *Forschungen zur Geschichte der kurialen Behörden vom Schisma bis zur Reformation* (2 vols., Rome, 1914); G. Barraclough, *Papal Provisions, Aspects of Church History, Constitutional, Legal and Administrative, in the Later Middle Ages* (Oxford, 1935); H. C. Lea, *A History of the Inquisition in the Middle Ages*, 3 vols. (New York, 1888); A. L. Maycock, *The Inquisition from its Establishment to the Great Schism* (London, 1927); J. Giraud, *L'Inquisition médiévale* (3rd edn., Paris, 1928); W. E. Lunt, *Papal Revenues in the Middle Ages*, 2 vols. (New York, 1934); Cl. Bauer, 'Die Epochen der Papstfinanz', HZ. CXXXVIII (1928), 457 sqq.; Cl. Bauer, 'Kirche, Staat und kapitalistischer Geist', AK XXI (1931), 151 sqq.; A. Schulte, *Der Adel und die deutsche Kirche im Mittelalter* (2nd edn., Stuttgart, 1922).

Tyrol, in employing the weapons of excommunication and
interdict to defend the out-of-date territorial rights of his episcopal
principality.

All this made the chances of appointing an efficient episcopate
very small. In Germany the monopoly of church places by the
nobility prevented this. When seeking admission to a cathedral
chapter it was usually more important than anything else to be
eligible to take part in tournaments and to boast eight or sixteen
quarterings. Even so, good men might be appointed; but
naturally that was far from usual. Noble bishops, frequently
even of princely families, whose election to an episcopal see made
them rulers of a secular principality, were mostly more concerned
to exploit the church and their congregations than to serve them.
Religious duties took second or even third place in their activities.
They had no effective contact with the faithful in their dioceses
and, especially in episcopal towns, where conditions produced
political and social unrest (see above, p. 114 sq.), the gap between
the ' shepherd ' and his ' flock ' was very wide.

Within the lower ranks of the clergy the main trouble lay in
their numbers, which far exceeded the numbers necessary to
perform their pastoral duties. There was no limit to the foundation and endowment of little chapels and special services by the
middle classes. Many of these may well have been acts of piety;
but frequently they were intended primarily to provide livings
for younger sons. And this was the main cause of the superfluity
of priests. Many town churches had dozens of these ' altar
priests ', ' mass priests ' and ' vicars ', as well as the usual parsons
and chaplains. There was no question of selection according to
merit or vocation. The consequences were shocking ignorance,
low moral standards, and economic misery among the vast
majority of the lower clergy. The only significant exceptions
were the clergy of the better parishes in the towns. It is no
exaggeration to speak of a ' clerical proletariat ', both in the
spiritual and in the material sense. Sebastian Brant called them
simply ' poor beasts ' (*armes viech*).

The people had little respect for clerics as a body, although
their reasons for disliking the lower clergy were not the same as
those which made them hate the higher clergy. Continual abuse

and criticism of clerical sins and shortcomings by men like Sebastian Brant, Geiler von Kaysersberg and Thomas Murner, who themselves never wavered in their allegiance to the church, were enough to shake such consideration and respect for the clerical calling as might still exist. The damage had already been done before the subversive and malicious Humanists came along.

A brief mention must also be made of the religious orders. They too, naturally, followed the general trend of the times. In the older orders, the Benedictines and the Cistercians, whose vast feudal estates required an appropriate administrative organization, the main trouble was the dominance of the nobility. The younger, mendicant orders, Dominicans and Franciscans, suffered because their ranks were overcrowded, and this led to a drastic lowering of their standards. In spite of the fact that a number of their members who excelled as popular preachers were the declared favourites of the masses, the dirty, stupid, hypocritical, braggart mendicant was the most despised character of the period.

But particularly in the older orders a serious, vigorous reform movement started about the beginning of the fifteenth century. It started in the monastery of Melk in Lower Austria and spread throughout the whole of southern Germany. Similarly the reform movement of Bursfeld (near Göttingen) spread via Benedictine and Windesheim congregations into all the Augustinian monasteries of north-west Germany. The ' Brothers of the Common Life ', protagonists of the *devotio moderna* (see below, p. 154 sqq.), were connected with the Augustinians, and they effected a genuine revival of religion and morals which had considerable effect on secular circles. Monks like those of Tegernsee, who were such enthusiastic followers of Nicholas of Cues, must have had high standards of morals and education. The same could be said of the Poor Clares in Nuremberg, who later, at the beginning of the Reformation, under the leadership of their abbess, Charitas Pirckheimer, stoutly resisted the chicaneries of the town council.

The vicar-general of Luther's order, Staupitz, was also an outstanding personality, sincerely religious and of high moral integrity. The Franciscans and Dominicans also produced some notable men and made positive efforts to reform their houses, but on the whole they lagged behind the older orders. Many monasteries and cloisters maintained standards of which there was no need to be ashamed right down to the end of the Middle Ages. Apart from the adherents of *devotio moderna*, however, their attempts to reform seem to have had very little effect outside the walls of their monasteries.

From the purely religious aspect the Papacy and the church lived on their fat for more than two centuries. They seemed to have inexhaustible reserves. There were complaints, protests and bitterness over this state of affairs. The church was not good enough, but it could not be abolished, for it controlled the only road to salvation. Yet a slow, subversive movement which was to undermine and destroy its authority was already under way, although it passed completely unnoticed by most contemporaries. Belief in the church and its remedies was no longer absolute. One warning signal was the first mass defection of a whole land, inspired by the heretical rising in Bohemia led by Hus, who was burned in 1415. The seed sown by the Hussite movement was propagated in many semi-secret, heretical conventicles in the German towns. About the end of the fifteenth century Germany was swept by a wave of hatred for Rome almost without parallel in history. Both in the upper and lower classes men's minds were open to the vehement threats of the wayward Ulrich von Hutten (d. 1523) against 'papists' and 'courtesans'. There followed the Reformation, by which in a very short time the authority of the church was completely broken—mainly by precisely the same middle-class elements as had been her ardent supporters and benefactors. We get the impression that it happened almost overnight! Such a rapid defeat would have been quite impossible if the church had really been in a sound, healthy condition.[1]

---

[1] Cf. A. Werminghoff, *Verfassungsgeschichte der deutschen Kirche im Mittelalter* (2nd edn., Leipzig/Berlin, 1913); E. Benz, *Ecclesia Spiritualis, Kirchenidee und Geschichtstheologie der franziskanischen Reformation* (Stuttgart, 1934); V. Redlich, *Tegernsee und die deutsche Geistesgeschichte im 15. Jahrhundert* (Munich, 1931); W. Kothe, *Kirchliche Zustände Strassburgs im 14. Jahrhundert* (Freiburg i. B., 1903); J. Gneven, *Die Kölner Karthause und die Anfänge der Katholischen Reform in Deutschland* (Münster, 1935); and for the different monastic reform movements of the fifteenth century, G. G. Coulton, *Five Centuries of Religion*, vol. IV (Cambridge, 1950).

THE POPULARIZATION OF RELIGION

The fact that theology had lost all power to inspire and reveal (see below, p. 147) is also a necessary premiss for a complete understanding of late mediaeval piety. The higher, intellectual representatives of the church no longer gave a lead in matters of religion. But lay society also had failed to produce an intellectual *élite* (as the knights had done) which might have led a religious revival. So the main current of development was decided by the mentality of the broad masses, including the lower clergy and the mendicant orders, whose standards were no higher than those of the common layman. Higher circles, both lay and clerical (with some exceptions, see p. 141), proved to be only too willing to follow the lead of the masses in this instance.

This was the first time that the ' people ' played any part in the history of German thought and religion. On the whole they were as pious as could be expected, and full of urgent religious longings. All manner of church ritual accompanied them from the cradle to the grave—and even beyond. Masses and blessings, the cult of saints and images, processions, pilgrimages, etc., were the weft of all public and private life. Sermons, above all moral sermons, had become the main activity of the church. Geiler von Kaysersberg once declared that mass without sermon was much more injurious to a congregation's faith than sermon without mass. Communal prayer in the family circle or in the workshop was taken for granted, and social and economic associations such as the guilds paid great attention to religious observances. Particularly in the fifteenth century people were desperately anxious to save their souls. ' Everybody was striving towards heaven ', was the brief explicit summing up of Burkard Zink, chronicler of Augsburg (d. 1474). There is a strong reflexion of the basic character of the period in this sentence: a highly charged religious atmosphere everywhere, and everybody excited and uneasy.

The late Middle Ages quite naturally followed paths in religion which had been embarked upon in the twelfth and thirteenth centuries. The main factors in question were the greater subjective awareness of people intensely interested in their personal salvation and the desire to give plastic and visible representation to the process (see above, p. 67 sq.). But the nervous energy peculiar to the later Middle Ages exaggerated all the trends deriving from these factors, and dissipated its efforts along all kinds of side-tracks and by-ways until it could no longer find a way back to the essentials of religion.

The forms of religious observance, particularly among the middle classes, were diverse and inconsequent. There was an endless confusion of extraordinary devotions; there were special saints and patrons for all communities and trades, for every illness, every earthly wish or vicissitude. There were innumerable fraternities and personal rituals. Their devotees were united in small, semi-private religious societies, which gave them the illusion of greater safety and intimate well-being than the orthodox church in the form of the parish community could offer. They were, as O. Clemen has said, *ecclesiolae in ecclesia*.[1]

The late Gothic town church was the typical, material expression of middle-class piety. The spacious hall of the nave was suitable for a large congregation around a preacher, whilst its fringes of chapels and altars in the side aisles, founded by different religious bodies or patrician families, provided for the special devotions of the *ecclesiolae* or ' little churches ' mentioned above. Both the moralizing trend in religion and the esoteric particularization of devotion led away from divine service in the centre of a united congregation towards the peripheries of religion.

Religious feeling and worship were dominated by a desire to make them intimate and private and to make holy features visible and material. The idea was to be surrounded with holiness, to have holiness ready to hand. God, the most elusive and ethereal of all concepts, was a most difficult subject for this kind of treatment and His Son could be approached only from the human side of His existence. But the Mother of God and the innumerable saints were human beings, with whom it was possible to speak and behave as humans. What was more important, they could be relied upon to intercede effectively

---

[1] O. Clemen, *Die Volksfrömmigkeit des ausgehenden Mittelalters* (Dresden/Leipzig, 1937), 7.

before God for human desires and interests, whether these concerned the life beyond or only daily life on earth. As a contemporary writer in Passau said, the faithful could not see the Saviour for saints.

Holy things were brought down to the level of the market-place and mingled with the gaudy ideas and feelings of the common people. They assumed pretty, idyllic forms; frequently they were treated as knick-knacks and toys; sometimes they were interpreted sentimentally or even sensually, but mostly they were proclaimed in the shrill tones of the neurotic blood-and-thunder naturalism which was part and parcel of middle-class life (see above, p. 130). There is ample evidence of this in contemporary pictures; in those comfortable, bourgeois bedrooms which form the inevitable background to the birth of Mary and many other familiar scenes from the legends of the saints. These, along with gruesome scenes of torture and martyrdom, the ' Man of Sorrows ', the dead body of Christ being shown to the people (*in der Wies*), or the Lady of Sorrows with her dead Son covered with wounds on her lap, were all new pictorial subjects in this period. Religious themes had to be worked into tumultuous crowd-scenes (Calvary, for instance), or set against naturalistic landscapes so that quite often nature seems no longer an auxiliary or a background to otherworldliness, but dominates and decides the form of the picture (see below, p. 146, fn. 2).

Even genuine, modest piety was spoiled by an admixture of coarse bad taste. Popular preachers did not hesitate to use the basest crudities in trying to strike the right note for the masses. Geiler von Kaysersberg, for instance, in a series of Easter sermons, told the story of Christ's sufferings in the allegory of making a cake. On another occasion he recommended the hare as an example for Christians; they should always fear God in the manner of the hare, whose lips constantly tremble and mumble; and if their ears were as long as his they would be able to hear the words of God all the better. And in the once so awe-inspiring mystery plays there was now too much trivial burlesque which was altogether unworthy of their religious themes. Saintly ladies were made to haggle with the hawker of ointments and his wife and servant. The disciples ran a wager to the grave, but failed to get there on account of an irresistible thirst! Devils, balked of their prey, dominated the scene of the Resurrection. Joseph had a passage of words with his maidservants and got a box on the ear from them. It was, indeed, the mentality of the masses that set the tone.

Anything intellectual or abstract had to be made visible and material at all costs. This was the reason for the insatiable demand for new miracles—especially when they could be connected with the Blood or the Body of Christ. People constantly sought out new places of pilgrimage—*currendi libido*, as it is called in the *Imitation of Christ*—where such things were to be seen. It was also the reason for the inexhaustible market for relics—not only relics of the saints, but also of Christ, Mary, the Apostles, the Three Kings and the patriarchs and prophets of the Old Testament. Collecting these holy objects had become a mania indulged in by everybody from members of small-town churches to rich patricians such as Nikolaus Muffel of Nuremberg, and even the Elector of Saxony, Frederick the Wise.

Obviously this led to a mercenary abuse of religion. Religious acts and rites were performed simply to secure certain advantages, both in heaven and on earth. This was particularly so in the worship of the saints, which was inspired entirely by the principle of ' give and it shall be given unto you '. Even the most fundamental rite of the church, mass, was pushed into the dark corners of religious practice; it was no longer regarded as an objective celebration of Christ's sacrifice for mankind. The participants expected some return, some practical *fructus* or *utilitates* (!) *missae*. They expected, for instance, that all their worldly affairs should go better and more smoothly on days on which mass was heard; or, that such days should not add to a man's age; or, that one should receive some special mercy from God, which He would otherwise have withheld, if one died on such a day. Votive masses to a particular saint, offered to gain some earthly privilege, and masses for the benefactor's soul became the most popular form of worship. And they were thought to be all the more certain to succeed if they were read in series of up to thirty masses—for each of which, of course, a certain number of candles and a sum of alms were required.

The observance of fixed conventions was an important factor in this popularized religion, which petrified into a rigid mould of formalities. Men very nearly succumbed to the temptation of trying to subjugate supernatural powers by means of fixed, formalized acts and prayers, which they believed to be infallible just because they were so formalized. They came, in fact, very near to practising magic in the name of religion. Cases of glaring misuse of the mass and the eucharist as instruments of sorcery were not rare, as is shown by the continual protests of the church against the practice.

The main aim was to make life safe and secure, both in this world and the next. This was the idea behind the multiplication of religious observances, the repetition of prayers, services, and good deeds and the membership of religious circles—all assessed on a purely quantitative basis. Indulgences made it possible to amass enormous credits of salvation. The Electors of Saxony had enough to guarantee immunity for something like two million years, and even when one of them had become the patron and protector of Luther, it was still considered insufficient! For the sake of 'safety' double confession at Easter became customary and was even demanded by the church, whereas for the rest of the year a single communion usually sufficed. Masses for a person's soul were accumulated indiscriminately. A rich burger of Enns had stored up 3,000 by 1495. In fifteen weeks, more than 9,000 masses were read for the Emperor Frederick III; and Charles V provided for 30,000 masses to save his soul. As A. L. Mayer put it, ' they took refuge in numbers '[1] as a substitute for confidence in God and His protection. This, perhaps more than anything else, shows how unstable was the basis of that anxious piety which sets the tone of the period.

In spite of all this they were capable of rising above things of the senses into intellectual, spiritual realms more suited to religion. This is proved by many beautiful popular hymns, such as ' Now let us pray to the Holy Ghost ' and ' Christ rose up to heaven ' (*Nu piten wir den heiligen geist* and *Christ fur gen himel*). Many confessionals and necrologies derived their faith and

---

[1] A. L. Mayer, ' Das Kirchenbild des ausgehenden Mittelalters und seine Beziehungen zur Liturgiegeschichte ', *Gedächtnisgabe O. Casel* (Düsseldorf, 1951), 292.

comfort directly from the thought of Christ's redemption of mankind and not from a belief in the intercession of saints or good works. Whether wholly or only partly translated into German the Bible was very popular. And those pictures of madonnas and saints, with such calm, composed expressions, cannot have been produced by a generation which was accustomed only to a nervous, materialistic distortion of religion.

But the unhealthy elements predominated. Religious thought and feeling were no longer the essential basis of Christian belief and practice. From the remote corners of religion to which they had been relegated they could still inspire simple minds with genuine religious feeling, and in fact every action of their daily life was given some kind of holy content. Nevertheless, through coarse familiarity with holy things (and with things of the devil!) the common man pulled the divine world down to his level until it had no power to influence him at all. Man formed God and all things divine in his own image and thus took away their true divine powers. There was no limit to the scope of debasement of this kind. Looked at from a genuine Christian point of view it was equivalent to a total, or at least a partial, relapse into paganism. Many far-seeing men, such as Gerson, d'Ailly, Cusanus, the author of the *Imitation of Christ*, and many official pronouncements of the church, sought to put a halt to these abuses, but they could do little against the will of the masses, supported as it was by the mendicant orders.[1]

Our reason for analysing in such detail the forms of worship of the late Middle Ages was to make clear that they were insufficient to continue to inspire social life for any length of time.

[1] On popular religion and piety, cf. J. Lortz, *Die Reformation in Deutschland*, Vol. I, (3rd edn., Freiburg, 1949); R. Pascal, *The Social Basis of the German Reformation* (London, 1933); L. A. Veit, *Volksfrommes Brauchtum und Kirche im deutschen Mittelalter* (Freiburg, 1936), with a wealth of material and a very detailed bibliography; St. Beissel, *Die Verehrung der Heiligen und ihrer Reliquien in Deutschland während des Mittelalters*, 2 vols. (2nd edn., Freiburg, 1892); A. Franz, *Die Messe im deutschen Mittelalter* (Frankfurt, 1902); P. Browe, 'Die Eucharistie als Zaubermittel im Mittelalter', AK. XX (1930), 134 sqq.; B. Smalley, *The Study of the Bible in the Middle Ages* (2nd edn., Oxford, 1952); A. L. Mayer, 'Das Kirchenbild des späten Mittelalters und seine Beziehungen zur Liturgiegeschichte', *Gedächtnisgabe O. Casel*, (Düsseldorf, 1951), 274 sqq.; A. L. Mayer, 'Die heilbringende Schau in Sitte und Kult', *Heilige Überlieferungen, Festgabe J. Herwegen* (Münster, 1938), 234 sqq. The two latter works open up new fields in our knowledge of the true nature of late mediaeval piety.

The often expressed desire for security shows that it did not exist. The general uncertainty of life is one of the most obvious characteristics of the Middle Ages in decline. Religious doubts were responsible for only a part of the general uneasiness, although it is certainly the part which is easiest to understand and describe. Political and social relationships were just as unstable. In time this uncertainty became a definite obsession: as J. Lortz said, ' Fear became a basic factor of the period ',[1] the pilgrimages of the Flagellants, pogroms against the Jews, children's pilgrimages, ready ecstatic response to sermons of repentance (the burning of ' vanities '), outbursts of mass hysteria at holy places, such as the pilgrimage to the Beautiful Maria in Regensburg, as represented in the well-known woodcut of Michael Ostendorfer—all these mass neuroses are symptoms of a general sense of fear. Fear of witches and witchcraft also started to spread in Germany in the first half of the fifteenth century. Particularly about the turn of the fifteenth and sixteenth centuries a spate of eschatological prophecies and ominous astrological forecasts of the future were very disturbing to contemporaries. They announced a stern judgement on Rome and the Papacy, or at least their imminent downfall. This was to be followed by a revolution which would destroy all existing political and social institutions, bringing a new religion and an altogether happy era. Durer's engravings (*Melancholy*; *Knight, Death and the Devil*; *The Secret Annunciation*), Grünewald's horrifying Crucifixion and his devils' masks on the Isenheim Altar, the surrealistic visions of the spirits of hell by Hieronymus Bosch—all bear witness to the feverish excitability of the period.

It would obviously be false to attempt to define the whole character of the late Middle Ages under this one heading. Not everybody was carried away by the popular wave of coarseness and fear; and many of those who were affected showed it in a completely different way. But it can be said quite definitely that by the turn of the fifteenth and sixteenth centuries society as a whole was neurotic and morbid. Riemenschneider and many other artists express nervous tension, suffering, and complete disillusionment very clearly. This is particularly evident in

---

[1] Lortz, *Die Reformation in Deutschland*, i, 100.

Riemenschneider's *Adam*, a youthful figure which nevertheless conveys an impression of bitterness and exhaustion in both his pose and his facial expression. Comparing this with the powerful, forthright man, showing no trace of responsibility for the burden of mankind, which represents Adam in the Cathedral of Bamberg (about 1240), one is aware of the distance covered in two hundred and fifty years in the history of the European soul.

It is difficult to arrange the contradictory light-and-shade elements of this confused epoch into a meaningful picture. But there is no doubt that the picture would be a sombre one. It must not be forgotten (above, p. 136) that the sudden, complete defection represented by the Reformation was completed in less than ten years. This is conclusive proof that there was something wrong with the outlook of the times—particularly with the religious outlook. For a sound and healthy society, certain of its aims, does not give up without a struggle all the things it worships, simply because a rebellious monk gives the signal to destroy them.[1]

THE THINKERS OF THE LATE MIDDLE AGES

Contemporary with, but a little removed from, these popular manifestations the intellectuals went their own way. Mysticism and the philosophical *via moderna* represented by Occamism were the main channels. Little as the two seem to have in common, they do finally converge into a single line in the history of thought. Both constitute a reaction against the confident intellectualism of Scholasticism at its peak and both turn their attention to the individual.

As H. Meyer demonstrated,[2] the *Summa* of the Scholastics was a rounded-off codification of all existing knowledge which signified the end of an intellectual epoch. Everything that could be attained by contemporary means and methods of abstract

---

[1] For the above, cf. J. Hansen, *Zauberwahn, Inquisition und Hexenprozesse im Mittelalter* (Munich/Leipzig, 1900); J. Hansen, *Quellen und Untersuchungen zum Hexenwahn* (Bonn, 1901); L. Thorndike, *History of Magic and Experimental Science*, 4 vols. (New York, 1923–1934); L. Weiser-Aall, 'Hexe', in *Handwörterbuch des deutschen Aberglaubens*, ed. E. Hoffmann-Krayer and H. Bächtold-Stäubli (10 vols., Berlin/Leipzig, 1927–42), Vol. III, cols. 1827–1920; W. E. Peuckert, *Die grosse Wende. Das apokalyptische Säkulum und Luther* (Hamburg, 1948).

[2] H. Meyer, *Geschichte der abendländischen Weltanschauung* iii, (Würzburg, 1948), 20.

thinking was included in it. But the definitive character of the great *Summae* was largely illusory. New problems arose; there was no halting-place. The nature of intellect itself was the most urgent problem of the fourteenth century. Philosophers now asked themselves whether man's logical powers of perception and expression really extended so far as the Scholastics had supposed. The system produced by the clear-thinking English Franciscan, William of Occam, who died in 1349 in Munich at the court of Louis of Bavaria, gave an emphatic, negative answer to this question.

Recent research into Occam's works shows that a great deal of it is still controversial, but it is generally accepted that Occam's nominalism denies real, independent existence to all general concepts. He regards them simply as auxiliaries, or a means of intellectual ready-reckoning. In this way he limited the province of perception, at least so far as controllable statements are concerned, to single facts which are empirically demonstrable. Hence metaphysical and theological spheres of activity were closed to the human intellect. Both the scholastics and those who preceded them (see above, p. 90) had been absolutely convinced of the prestabilized harmony of the universe and of the teleological purpose behind the progress of this world. All this was now invalidated and thinkers could no longer perceive any purpose or logic in the world about them. It could not be proved that belief in revelation was reasonable—it simply had to be believed. Even the concepts of ' good ' and ' evil ' could not be categorical absolutes, anchored in the very nature of God, and so morality was not the product of reason but of God's commandments and prohibitions.

Occam developed the ' Voluntarism ' of Duns Scotus (d. 1308), who had first propounded the view that God was a completely arbitrary power consisting of nothing but volition. This meant that good and evil are decided entirely by divine prescription. If God, for instance, had demanded that we should hate one another, perhaps even Him also, then hatred would have been good and love wicked. God was above and beyond human understanding, entirely arbitrary, and with a strong tendency towards the God of punishment and revenge of the Old Testament.

L

One consequence of this nominalistic ' liberation of the mundane from God '[1] was the strong impulse it gave to empirical science. Experimental science, which had been eagerly taken up by Albertus Magnus, and then, more purposefully, by the English Franciscan Roger Bacon (d. 1294) and his followers, became much more important from the fourteenth century onwards. It took the forms of chemistry, alchemy, magnetism, optics, laws of gravity, etc. The Scholastics, even in the days of their greatness, had completely ignored all this. Nevertheless the spell of the old, largely Aristotelian, philosophic observation of nature was not completely broken. Great revolutionary discoveries in science do not belong to the Middle Ages.[2]

Nominalism and Voluntarism converged on a decided irrationalism and agnosticism in metaphysics and ethics. For the second time in the history of mediaeval thought, belief and rational knowledge were divorced. But whilst Averroism (see above, p. 96)—which survived sporadically into the later Middle Ages—regarded the two as hostile opposites, Occamism treated them as two separate spheres which have nothing to do with each other. Carried to its logical conclusions Occamism would atomize human perception. In practice it brought a strong element of doubt and uncertainty into the foundations of learning, morals and religion.

This was true, at any rate in principle. Most of the philosophy and theology of the late Middle Ages was influenced by Occamism. But Occam's less able followers modified their master's opinions and brought them back on to orthodox ecclesiastical lines, employing all kinds of sophistry to render his teaching innocuous. The extent of Occam's influence on the late fourteenth

---

[1] H. Meyer, *op. cit.*, 321.

[2] The increasing importance of nature in painting, which went hand in hand with this interest in the natural sciences, can only be treated very briefly here. It started with Giotto, about 1300, who placed *living* people against realistic landscapes whilst yet maintaining the sacred, awe-inspiring effect of the picture. The development was slow and it proved difficult to dispense with artificial backgrounds of gold-leaf; and so, after Giotto, no decisive progress can be seen before the fifteenth century. But from then on perspective and distinctions between foreground and background became more important in sacred pictures and, indeed, frequently came to dominate the whole. In the transition to the modern era studies of exclusively natural subjects or landscapes without persons became general—Dürer, Altdorfer, Wolf, Huber.

and fifteenth centuries has not yet been fully assessed, but it seems as though it is not to be dismissed lightly. In particular it seems probable, even if as yet not proved, that Occam's conception of an unpredictable, autocratic God influenced the theological education of the parish priests, and so strengthened the general popularization of religion. It was yet another reason for exaggerated fears of personal damnation which had to be insured against by worshipping saints and accumulating good deeds. Even Luther in his early days acquired some traces of a much diluted Occamism from the works of the last noteworthy representative of the school, Gabriel Biel (d. 1495). So there was a little truth in his assertion that he was an Occamist.

Germany merely kept in step with the general European development. It had at last caught up with the intellectual progress of other countries as a result of the foundation of a number of universities from 1348 onwards. And there was plenty of active interest in knowledge. But learning, like every other activity of the period, split up into innumerable small branches and so lost its power to influence society as a whole. There were Thomists, Albertists, Scotists and Occamists, and none of them ever had a clear idea as to how they differed from one another. The trade in learning led them round and round in pompous circles in a desert of petty distinctions and pedantic quarrels. As the revolutionary effects of Luther's teachings were soon to show, the real problems of philosophy and religion, which should have been the concern of the period, remained untouched, if not completely unrecognized. And so people became more and more estranged from the learned ' cowled monks and theologizers ', as Johann Eck himself called them. According to the humanistic Dominican Johannes Faber, writing in 1520, the world was ' tired of the gymnastics of theological sophistry and thirsty for the springs of evangelical truth '.[1]

[1] On the philosophical movements, cf. G. de Lagarde, *La naissance de l'esprit laique au déclin du moyen âge* (4 vols., Saint-Paul-Trois-Chateaux, 1934–42), Vol. IV: *Ockham et son temps*; C. H. Haskins, *Studies in the History of Medieval Science* (1924); P. Duhem, *Le système du monde de Platon à Copernic*, 5 vols. (Paris, 1913–1917); W. Ganzenmüller, 'Alchemie und Religion im Mittelalter ', DA. V (1942), 372 sqq.; G. Ritter, *Die Heidelberger Universität*, Vol. I (Heidelberg, 1936); G. Ritter, ' Studien zur Spätscholastik ', *Sitzungsberichte der Heidelberger Akademie der Wissenschaften*, 1921, 1922, 1926–7; G. Ritter, ' Romantische und revolutionäre Elemente in der deutschen

There was just one man who alone might have steered learning out of the dreary maze of its own subtleties. This was Cusanus (Nicholas of Cues, 1401–64), probably the most brilliant thinker of the Middle Ages. His rather dubious activities in church politics would seem to indicate that he was merely a child of his time, but his philosophical works might have prompted a new and more fruitful epoch in academic philosophy if they had not been fated to lie fallow for so long.

According to him, God, the universe and all living things are indivisible, essential elements of the general structure of life. The universe and all things in it constitute the *explicatio*, the ' externality ' of God, who is the absolute *implicatio*, the internal nature, of all things. ' God gave Himself to us in the form of the visible and tangible world, so that it might exist for His sake. . . . God is in everything and everything is in Him '. Man's mind, an original picture of God's mind, by its very nature contains the whole of non-human creation and only needs to evoke it in its thoughts. He is equally both *humanatus Deus* and *humanus mundus*. And the more man exerts his mind to ' unfold ' nature in this manner ' the richer will be his fertility within himself '. Cusanus did not found all this on speculation alone but sought support for it in his own extensive scientific observations and experiments. In seeking to understand the world—which for him implies active, creative participation in it—man is called upon to help in the implementation of God's intention, because man, as representative of the Almighty, raises not only himself but all material things to the supreme ' peace in God '. So it is by way of the universe, and not by segregating himself from it, that man must realize himself in God. ' To have understood the art of the Almighty, which created the ages of the world and all life, and even reason . . . is to have entered into the company of the sons of God (*filiatio*) and into inheritance of the eternal kingdom '. By fulfilling his destiny on earth man decides his fate in heaven; this means that his cultural activity is invested with religious

Theologie am Vorabend der Reformation ', VLit. V (1927), 342 sqq.; H. Heimsoeth *Die sechs grossen Themen der abendländischen Metaphysik und der Ausgang des Mittelalters* (2nd edn., Breslau, 1934); F. W. Oediger, *Über die Bildung der Geistlichen im späten Mittelalter* (Leiden/Cologne, 1953).

significance. It also makes man's task absolutely endless, because 'intellectual vision is never sated with the contemplation of truth, for our power to see becomes continually sharper and stronger'. As our powers of perception are constantly changing and progressing, a final, comprehensive *summa* of knowledge is impossible. Every single individual has his own particular obligations towards himself, humanity and the universe, and he cannot delegate them. For the individual's participation in God's perfection is unique and non-recurring, and he must exercise this inherent participation in full. Only as a member of the whole can he become truly individual, and the whole of creation can fulfil its basic nature only through the self-realization of the individual. Such is God's purpose. He says to man: ' Be yourself and of yourself; strive after true self-realization—and then I shall be yours '. Once again it is a case of religion being inextricably mixed up with worldly individualism and optimism.

Still working along the lines of philosophic speculation Cusanus arrived at spectacular results in cosmology. He decided that the earth is not the centre of the universe: in fact such a thing is impossible, for it is merely a star among other stars and there is probably life on the others. The earth moves (as also do the fixed stars) and its shape is almost spherical. In God all opposites are reconciled (*coincidentia oppositorum*), but it is a basic law governing this world that it exists only through the conflict of opposites which are inherent in man's limitations and imperfections as an individual. This is the reason why there can be no ' proportion ' or ' analogy ' between finite and infinite. Everything that takes place in this world is the product of the eternal interaction of contingencies and different external forms. ' The beginning of one thing constitutes the decline of another. . . . Death seems to be nothing but the dissolution of a structure into its component elements '. The universe is a constant quantity composed of materials and forces which are always changing under their mutual influences. Here Cusanus arrived at absolutely fundamental perceptions which changed the static philosophy of the Scholastics into principles of dynamic progress; if they had been followed up, they would have inaugurated a completely new approach to both the physical and the intellectual aspects of the world. At the same time they demonstrate forcibly that man's search for truth and knowledge is interminable.

Even the methods of Cusanus's thought were quite new. Although definitely related to Plato, the Neoplatonists and the mystics in his approach, he stands out quite distinct from them in certain essential features. He alone denied categorically that the individual and concrete manifestations of God's creation are inferior in value, as all previous systems had maintained. Believing that these individual entities were part of the divine being, he really felt them to be of supreme importance. In addition, unlike the Scholastics, he went beyond the limits imposed by purely conceptual and dialectic thinking. He considered that a *prima seu mentalis philosophia* was more important than Aristotelian *rationalis philosophia*. By the former he meant that the human mind (in the image of the Divine Mind) searching its own depths, rises above the generally accepted laws of rational thought which are capable of dealing with only a limited field of speculation. And this subjective speculation could, with the help of mathematical, abstract concepts, make clear many things which could not be expressed in the terms of conceptual logic. It was all a matter of following up instinctive convictions—'as a retriever finds its game with certainty but without knowledge'. This was the *docta ignorantia* of Cusanus, inspired by infinite optimism and faith in the 'power of the spiritual nature of man, the highest after God'.

Such bold speculations opened up endless philosophical perspectives to Cusanus. But he remained alone in his greatness and belonged to no 'school' or university. The Scholastics—and not only his contemporaries among them—either ignored his work or attacked it bitterly as being 'pantheistic'. Even the humanists, who could have found in it so much that was congenial to them, neither took him seriously nor really understood him. It is yet another sign of the impotence of this moribund age that men could not even begin to understand the only contemporary genius.[1]

[1] Cf. E. Vansteenberghe, *Le Cardinal Nicolas de Cues* (Paris, 1920); E. Hoffmann, *Nikolaus von Cues* (Heidelberg, 1947); M. de Gandillac, *Nikolaus von Cues, Studien zu seiner Philosophie und philosophischen Weltanschauung* (Düsseldorf, 1953); M. Seidlmayer, 'Zur Religionsauffassung des Nikolaus von Cues; AK. XXXVI (1954), 145 sqq.

MYSTICISM

Mysticism was the second movement which influenced and helped to define the intellectual nature of the last three hundred years of the Middle Ages. Its origins lay in the 'primitive mysticism' of Bernard of Clairvaux (see above, p. 66 sq.) and the school of St. Victor in Paris, which was more philosophical in its approach. From the thirteenth century onwards mysticism was very strong in Germany, particularly among the ladies in the cloisters and the beguines. The latter were pious, semi-religious societies, living a communal life in the so-called *beguinages*, but without taking any religious vows.[1] An early lead was given by the Thuringian nunnery of Helfta, which housed the great women mystics, Mechthild of Magdeburg (d. 1283), Mechthild of Hackeborn (d. 1299) and Gertrude the Great (d. 1302). All these women yearned passionately for a mystical experience of God. Mechthild of Magdeburg gave the name ' Jubilus ' to the fulfilment of such experience and described it as a state of emotion in which she could bear witness to her burning love for God ' in a voice too beautiful to be human, but not in meaningful words '.

As early as 1250 this came to be known as the ' new art '. Its aim was direct communion and unity of the soul with God. It could be, and for the most part was, sought within the framework of the usual church doctrines and practices, which directed mystical feeling towards Jesus Christ. But, as it was founded on individual experience, it was prone to break out of this framework. As A. L. Mayer said,[2] the medium of the priest and the sacraments was not rejected, but in the last and decisive instance, it was not considered; it was swallowed up more or less completely in a mystical twilight. Adelheid Langmann, a nun, prayed to God, 'If You have any love at all for me, then come to me Yourself, instead of just sending messengers '. Again, as A. L. Mayer pointed out, it was to a large extent the desire to get away from the material-minded, mercenary church which drove people to look for a direct, personal way to God. As was natural, the church at

[1] Cf. E. W. McDonnell, *The Beguines and Beghards in Medieval Culture* (Rutgers Univ. Press, 1954).
[2] Mayer, *Kirchenbild*, 290–291.

first regarded the movement with considerable suspicion; but then, in the words of H. Grundmann, 'it broke into the old preserves of the church in successive waves directed from a single source, until finally the church was able to defend itself only by admitting these new forms of piety into its own constitution and giving them room to expand'.[1]

There were more than eighty houses of Dominican nuns in Germany at the beginning of the fourteenth century, and the fact that the philosophy of their 'holy High Master, Brother Eckart', whom they revered and loved beyond measure, found its most fertile home there, is proof of their high intellectual standards. For the mysticism of Eckart (circa 1260-1327) is entirely devoid of those features of extravagant emotion and sweet heart's ease which made mysticism in general so attractive to the feminine temperament. His is not an emotional mysticism but a strict, speculative mysticism, which Eckart nevertheless intended should inspire and shape the practical life of his community.

The problems arising out of the numerous and often contradictory theories of Master Eckart, particularly the discrepancies between his scholastic works in Latin and his sermons in German, are for the most part still open questions. But it must be admitted that there is a strong element of pantheism in his mysticism, however emphatically he himself may have denied it. His postulate that the birth of the Son out of the Father and the creation of the world were parts of a single act of divine birth-giving was based entirely on Neoplatonism. Because of this everything in creation is to some extent divine, and Eckart continually emphasized this in different formulations: ' God is divine because He is one with all things '. This brought him into the dilemma of trying to reconcile the Neoplatonic theory of emanation and his own spiritualistic contempt for the material world. His solution was that things and beings in their individual state of existence are ' nothing at all ' (*das eine reine Nichts*); their one aim and desire is, and must be, to return to the being which gave them birth.

For Eckart God and the soul were everything; he could not come to any understanding of the material world. He saw a

[1] H. Grundmann, ' Die geschichtlichen Grundlagen der deutschen Mystik ', VLit. XII (1934), 410.

divine basis (in the fullest sense of the word) in the soul—the immanent ' little spark of the soul '. This is ' not only united with God but is a complete entity with Him ' and is not merely a state of being but a process of becoming, the pursuit of which is the foremost duty of man. Man's first task is ' to divest and be free of himself and all things '. This is naturally a rather painful process, but Eckart does not connect it in any way with ascetic denial—particularly of the body; it is exclusively a matter for the soul. God wishes to rule ' where all is bare ', ' in the primitive vales ', ' in the silent desert '. Under these conditions the climax, the birth of God in the soul, takes place. This is (Eckart is insistent on this point) exactly the same as the birth of the Son from the Father, and a person in whom it has come to pass is identical with the Son of God—' there is no difference between the Son born of His body and such a soul '. And God needs such people, in fact ' without them He would not know what to do ' (*er wüsste ohne ihn nicht, was tun*).

' Devote all your thoughts to the end that God may grow big within you ' (*darauff sez all din studieren daz dir Gott gross wird*)—the birth of God in the soul of man is everything. The traditional explanation of the birth of Christ, as the ' Mediator ' and the complete, once offered agent of deliverance from all our sins, is not affected by this. But Eckart maintains that these beliefs are of minor importance compared with this rebirth in the soul. God does everything directly, without any agency. Eckart did not attack the power of the church's keys to salvation, the sacraments; but he implied that they have no decisive power and, in the last instance, are not necessary.

After Eckart had been posthumously condemned by the church, his most important disciples, Johannes Tauler (d. 1361) and Heinrich Seuse (Suso, d. 1366), were careful to whittle down all those points of his teachings which offended against orthodox dogma. They retained, however, the main point, that the unity of God and the soul was real and factual, not simply a symbol or a ' moral lesson ' as in the teaching of Bernard of Clairvaux. For the rest Seuse kept well away from lofty speculation in Eckart's manner. It was through Seuse that soulful passion was re-established as the dominant element of mysticism, and the desire to illustrate inner experience in material, pictorial form. In particular Seuse used the idiom of courtly love-poetry, and described his own life and efforts as feudal service to his heavenly lady, i.e. ' eternal wisdom '. Similarly, the particular form of the cult of the Virgin Mary which he encouraged was strongly tinged with courtly romanticism. With all his poetic depth of feeling Seuse frequently drags things down to a very earthly level; he indulges in playful arabesques of style and dissolves into tearful sentimentality. The higher flights of mysticism were past and the popularization of the movement was under way.

Eckart's mysticism, like that of his contemporaries and his predecessors, had been disciplined and clearly outlined; and he always addressed himself to the ' homo nobilis '. But after his death the movement was debased and led into a maze of side-tracks. Even in the mysticism practised in the nunneries there was a lot of unhealthy sentimentality and religious sensualism, concentrating on Jesus and His Mother. Heinrich von Nörd-lingen and his soul-mate Margarethe Ebner (d. 1351) offer typical examples of this. Along with some very worthy and pious teaching these degenerate trends were passed on to the masses by a tremendous spate of religious literature. For example, one writer, a cleric, recommended the contemplation of the physical details of Mary's body and described how he had frequently been comforted with her milk. Furthermore, the movement branched off into channels which were frankly heretical. The ' Brothers and Sisters of Free Thought ' (*Brüder und Schwestern des freien Geistes*) formed circles in Swabia and in the Rhineland. The community of ' Friends of God ', which grew up around Rulman Merswin (d. 1382), a pupil of Tauler, on the Upper Rhine, seems to have kept just within the bounds of orthodoxy.

Mysticism was introduced to the Netherlands by Jan van Ruysbroeck (d. 1381), after Eckart the finest speculative thinker of his day. In the Low Countries the movement enjoyed an Indian summer of some importance. For the circle grew into the ' Brothers of the Common Life ' (*Fraterherren* or *Brüder vom gemeinsamen Leben*), one of the innumerable religious sects which arose out of the general uneasiness of the late Middle Ages. This society became the fountain head of *devotio moderna*, which must be regarded as the most important religious revival of the late Middle Ages, mainly because it spread so widely into secular society.

It matters very little whether we consider *devotio moderna* to be a branch of the very wide movement which goes under the name of Mysticism or not. The existence of the name itself shows that contemporaries regarded it as something distinct.[1] And *devotio moderna* had nothing in common with the heaven-storming fervour of the true philosophic mystics, who tried to plumb the deepest secrets of life and who, after they had proceeded from God to the world of nature and then back to God, were convinced that it was possible to become united in ' a single being ' with the Absolute Divinity. The adherents of *devotio moderna* also kept aloof from the current fashion of bringing God down to the level of man and illustrating all religious experience with cheap material symbols. They pursued a quiet life of devotion combined with a very practical moral code, which, although they were energetic educators, eliminated everything that might be detrimental to the virtues of *simplicitas cordis*, *humilitas* and *paupertas*, in the sense in which they were to be understood from the Sermon on the Mount. The movement anticipated many characteristics of Pietism and the narrow, fearful Quietism of succeeding centuries. Their ideals were tenderness of heart and appreciation of the *dulcedo Dei*, which showed itself especially in their intensive, eucharistic piety. As Stadelmann has put it, they replaced the vision of God of the mystics by a visitation of God (*visitatio Sanctissimi*). All this is to be seen quite clearly in the *Imitatio Christi* of Thomas à Kempis (d. 1471), the most comprehensive account of *devotio moderna*. And because it was the first consideration of its leaders to concentrate on the essentials of religion, to purify and simplify religious practice, they took the lead in the fight against the extravagances and exaggerations and all the symptoms of presumptuous sensationalism in religion, which had become so widespread and popular.

Their ideal of pious contemplation sprang from a strong

---

[1] Terms like ' the new art ', ' via moderna ', ' devotio moderna ' are worthy of notice; the people of the late Middle Ages themselves were aware that they were leaving behind their old allegiances, forms and standards.

individualistic trend. It was intended to produce a more personal, subjective approach and so make people more independent in their approach to religious ethics. Previously individual consciences had been guided and ruled by the priesthood, but now the influence of the priest was considerably weakened. Along these lines *devotio moderna* made some steps at least towards a solution of what J. Lortz called ' one of the basic problems of the age: recognition of the fact that the Christian congregation had come of age ',[1] which otherwise the late Middle Ages had overlooked to their detriment. But the nature of the movement as a whole made it acceptable to one type of mind only—the mind eager to find a pietistic solution. Nor was it ever widespread geographically; and so it failed to make any decisive impression on the general development of the period. Nevertheless it helps us to see why, at a later date, Luther's tract *On the Freedom of the Christian* had a far greater impact than any other of his writings —even in circles which were declared supporters of the old church.[2]

HUMANISM

Of the new intellectual and religio-ethical movements mentioned above (p. 111), which mark the transition to the modern age, the only further one which can be said to belong to the Middle Ages is Humanism.

In his *Confessions* St. Augustine had said: ' Man is a bottomless pit . . . the hairs of his head are easier to count than the desires and emotions of his heart '—' I myself do not know quite what

---

[1] Lortz, *Reformation* i, 56, 121.

[2] On the mystics cf. J. Bernhart, *Die philosophische Mystik des Abendlandes* (Munich, 1922)—a most penetrating introduction; H. Grundmann, ' Die geschichtlichen Grundlagen der deutschen Mystik ', VLit. XII (1934), 400 sqq.; H. Grundmann, *Religiöse Bewegungen im Mittelalter* (Berlin, 1935); X. de Hornstein, *Les grands mystiques allemands du XIVe siècle*, 2 vols. (4th edn., Paris, 1924); J. Bernhart, *Der Frankfurter (Theologia teutsch)* (Munich, n.d.); J. A. Bizet, *Seuse et le déclin de la Scholastique* (Vol. I: Paris, 1945); J. Kuckhoff, *Johann von Ruysbroeck* (Munich, 1938); W. Öhl, *Deutsche Mystikerbriefe von 1001-1550* (Munich, 1931); A. Dempf, *Meister Eckhardt* (Leipzig, 1934); E. Seeberg, *Meister Eckhardt* (Tübingen, 1934); M. A. Lücker, *Meister Eckhardt und die Devotio moderna* (Leiden/Cologne, 1950); J. M. Clark, *The Great German Mystics, Eckhart, Tauler and Suso* (Oxford, 1949); P. Mestwerdt, *Die Anfänge des Erasmus, Humanismus und ' Devotio moderna '* (Leipzig, 1917), a fundamental work; H. Nottarp, ' Die Brüder vom gemeinsamen Leben ' Sav. VI (*kan. Abteilung* XXXII, 1943), 384 sqq.

I am '. When Petrarch (d. 1374) ' discovered ' and proclaimed this aspect of the genius of Augustine, whose spiritual depth and passion were beyond the comprehension of the Middle Ages, he revealed a new kind of humanity to his contemporaries. There had obviously been a long period of preparation for this change. The extent to which the truly mediaeval attitude of ' keeping men from thinking about themselves ' (Maritain), had been relaxed both in secular and religious matters, has been described above. Men had started to look into their own hearts and minds. But as Burckhardt said, it was Humanism which finally destroyed the veil under which man's consciousness had lain dreaming or half-awake. Although still deep in the Middle Ages, 'modern man ' was advancing on to the stage.

Life for its own sake and the variety of its challenges to their intelligence attracted and stimulated the Humanists more than any previous generation. They saw the life of every individual as something unique, something which could never be re-enacted or repeated. That was the ideal which everybody should try to realize. The words from Hölderlin's poem *Brot und Wein*, ' We are all looking for an individuality of our own, however far away it may be ', might serve as a motto for the whole of the Humanist movement. Petrarch said, ' I am an individual and would like to be wholly and completely an individual; I wish to remain true to myself, so far as I can '.

From this moment onwards men were for ever attuning their ears to themselves; eavesdropping on every movement of their inner selves and their reactions to stimuli from outside. And all that they discovered in the process had to be brought out into the light for examination, so that it could be cultivated and refined. Everything that had to do with their inner selves was of the greatest importance, and consequently it had to be passed on to others who were like-minded. Their introspection was given a safety-valve in the form of regular, personal confession to friends and the public. Their approach to life has been described as ' ethical individualism ', but ' ethical and aesthetic individualism ' would probably be a better description. Petrarch has come to be regarded as the prototype of this kind of Humanism—and indeed no other contemporary seems to have carried it quite so far as he. G. Voigt said of him, ' his greatest, most arduous and most meritorious achievement was himself '.

Books and learning, nature, love, friendship, and all aspects of life, even religion, had to have one focal point—the ego. The value of all things was decided on the basis of whether or no it elevated or served or helped to assert the ego in question.

The same considerations applied to the revival of the ancient world—' digging out the forgotten and almost buried letters from the underworld ', as Rudolf Agricola wrote in praise of Petrarch. The imposing thought and worldly wisdom as well as the formal elegance of the ancient poets and orators provided ideal models for the Humanists. They were the embodiment of those *bonae litterae* or *artes humanitatis* without which no balanced and full personality could come to maturity. For they did not offer knowledge alone—they formed and polished a man's personality as a whole, mind and soul, temperament and taste.

The Humanists could do nothing, however, with the learning of their own day; it isolated the mind from man's other faculties and attributes and left the rest to decay. The sterile, ponderous form—or, rather, the disregard of form and style—of contemporary letters was an offence against any Humanist's aesthetic feeling. So the Humanists started their fight against the ' deranged and wildly howling pack of Scholastics ' (Petrarch), and the same quarrel prompted in Germany the abusive *Epistolae Obscurorum Virorum*. Nevertheless the Humanists adopted many features of scholasticism and much that was derived straight from Aristotle. There is ample proof of this in the *Camaldulensian Disputes* of Christofforo Landino, one of the most typical products of Humanism. In Italy there was an imposing company of students and followers of Aristotle; in Germany Agricola wrote his *Inventio dialectica*; and Jakob Wimpfeling even went so far as to defend the Scholastics. And there were many more instances, for even Humanists were reluctant, and in fact unable, to dispense entirely with scholastic learning. They only demanded that it should be made to keep its proper place in their ambition to reach their ideal concept of the *artes humanitatis*.

They were so whole-hearted in pursuing their new cult of personality that all connexions with the external, material world seemed to be downright hindrances. The great yearning of the Humanists, as expressed by Poggio (d. 1459), was *sibi soli vacare*—to be free for oneself alone. Petrarch gave a personal example of the *vita privata et solitaria* which he preached in his writings. He barricaded himself against the outer world in the rural peace and quiet of his little, self-sufficing villa at Vaucluse; this was his *arx munitissima*, his ' safe, quiet and happy haven '. Not that he wished to renounce and deny the world outside like a monk, but he wanted to control the dose himself and take it only in a purified, and therefore artificial, form.

Once more (see above, pp. 67, 80, 83 sq., 105) the old forms of religious asceticism helped to stimulate this renewed urge to participate more fully in the life of this world. The *vita solitaria* of Petrarch and his successors was modelled in most details on the life of monks and hermits—certainly in everything that had to do with discipline of mind and body. But step by step and almost imperceptibly they deprived it of its religious purpose and substituted worldly standards.

The *vita privata* became the ambition of all Humanists, whether north or south of the Alps. Agricola saw in Petrarch, the *libertatis suae amator*, his own ideal. Willibald Pirckheimer, on losing his wife after only seven years of marriage, admitted freely that he now had one major duty of his (patrician) rank behind him, and had no intention of allowing the freedom which he so badly needed to be curtailed again. Mutianus Rufus shut himself up in Gotha in his *secura et vere beata tranquillitas*. In his *Convivium religiosum* Erasmus painted a charming picture of an ideal life of privacy, and explained, ' If I am to live at all I must live for myself . . . , for life is no life for me without this freedom '. They all aspired to own a country villa to which they could retire from time to time, either completely alone or with a few chosen friends. The obligations associated with a permanent residence, family life, regular professions were to be avoided, because they threatened that freedom so essential to self-development. Homelessness, uneasiness, distaste for 'bourgeois' ways of living, all show quite clearly both their strong emotions and the inner uncertainty with which they set out on a new kind of life.

What is more, it was a life lacking a solid foundation in society.

As both Petrarch and Agricola came to learn, it failed to bring the inner peace and personal satisfaction for which they longed. It tried to ignore man's inevitable dependence on the world around him. For the first time in our period society and the individual were consciously and in principle opposed to one another. This was an exciting problem and it became one of the main themes of the Humanists' discussions about the complete life. When they argued about the respective merits of the *vita activa* and the *vita contemplativa* they reverted to the old clerical terms; but the concepts were not the same, for they invested these words with middle-class social and political content. There was considerable political tension in Humanist circles in Italy, where the old ideal of the autonomous city-state, mainly exemplified by Florence, had a hard fight against the ideology of tyranny, which tried to force the ordinary citizen to accept a passive role in political matters. First one party and then the other seemed to gain a decisive lead, but on the whole the outcome was a superficial and unsatisfactory compromise.

In the opinion of the Florentine, Alberti (d. 1472), expressed in the *Camaldulensian Disputes*, the true man ' should strive in his secluded retreat to participate in the greatest good, and should act in such a manner that no harm can come to him or his kin '— a rather weak, pragmatic standpoint, implying that one should partly relinquish one's true purpose in life in the interests of the community. Their ego was, as a rule, too strong to permit them to reach a solution which did justice to both the individualistic and the social sides of their natures. Only a very few, such as the noble pedagogue Vittorino da Feltre (d. 1446), and his pupil Federigo da Montefeltre or, north of the Alps, the English chancellor Thomas More (d. 1535), achieved any real balance in this respect. And these were successful mainly because they adhered to traditional Christian principles. At the height of the Italian Renaissance the famous *Courtier* of Count Baldassare Castiglione (d. 1529) presented the ideal figure of a courtier; he should be a man of this world, completely secularized, in whom every personal quality must harmonize smoothly with his duty towards state and society. But Castiglione's picture is rationalized and artificial, and is not, therefore, a very convincing ideal. The example of the *Courtier*, adapted to national character, and made a little more sober and conservative, produced the ideal of the gentleman in England; and here, and nowhere else, the cult of individual personality was subordinated to the ideal of public service. In France, and even more in Germany, the cult of the *vita privata* prevailed; the result was to emphasize the dichotomy of personality that was inherent in Humanism. Montaigne (d. 1592) defined it in the classic phrase: ' Montaigne and the mayor have always been two different men '. And Pirckheimer, for instance, the powerful senator of Nuremberg, might have said the same. It is fully explained by Erasmus in his *Colloquium senile*, in the remark of an old man who said that he had chosen a public office ' which carries enough prestige to save me from public contempt, for nobody can reproach me with living for myself alone . . . but which makes very few demands on me '.

How could this new concept of *Humanitas* be compatible with religious belief? In spite of the fact that several Humanists wore clerical garb the movement really represented an intellectual rising of the secular middle classes. But as we have seen, this lay society had always been uneasy and uncertain in its attitude to the ascetic, clerical view of life. Humanism had thus the task of creating its own code of religious ethics—one which would genuinely satisfy its demands. Even in this field they had to look for something individual. But in the last resort the religious ethical theme of Humanism was that very problem of Christian freedom for the laity which we have mentioned above—how to recognize that the Christian had come to maturity.

The endless fulminations of the Humanists against monks and clerics were motivated not so much by any real or imagined decadence and laxity in the monasteries, nor by the incurable dialectical aggressiveness of the Humanists, but represented rather a reaction, conscious or unconscious, against the existing narrow-minded conception of Christianity, which considered that any man who was not a monk was not religious. Erasmus, who had been a monk himself, asserted in his *Enchiridion militis Christiani* (a primer of Christian knowledge for laymen) that *monachatus non est pietas*—meaning that a man does not automatically become more pious when he becomes a monk.

M

It is well known that the Humanists' eager interest in actual topical aspects of life led them to flirt with pagan trends and fashions. This was particularly the case in Italy from the fifteenth century onwards; there was relatively little of it in Germany. In fact, with very few exceptions men pretended to be far more heathen—or less Christian—than they really were, or even wanted to be. Nearly all those 'free-thinkers' with their superior manner and scintillating arguments were 'converted' on their death-beds or before. As far as religion was concerned, the most serious problem with which the Humanists had to deal shows up more in their attempts to be thoroughly Christian than in their free-thinking and pseudo-heathen fashions.

On the whole they desired nothing more than a gentle equilibrium between the *Humanum* (as they understood it) and the *Divinum*. In their view, education in the 'humane arts' and close study of the Bible showed the way to true piety—a piety equally free of all paganism and of all the 'Judaic' elements of formalistic, dogmatic religion. Such studies should lead to a simple, ethical way of life and hence to true happiness and salvation. Erasmus considered that genuine Christian piety could be taught and learned: 'I have tried to produce a kind of text-book of piety, just as another man might try to write a text-book of a given science'. Christ was for him the supreme teacher; 'He is an example to us, embodying all the basic principles (*rationes*) of a happy life'. In fact Erasmus regarded Him as the true Epicurean, and 'there are no greater Epicureans than Christians who lead a pious life, for nobody lives pleasurably if he does not live piously'. Moral philosophy in the form of worldly wisdom and theology were fused together in a *pia quaedam philosophia*, as Marsiglio Ficino (d. 1499) described his *Theologia Platonica*, or, as Erasmus termed it, simply a *philosophia Christi*. The piety of the Humanists turned into an 'educative religion', whose ultimate aim was to teach people to lead a full life on earth. Through this process the Christian *Divinum* was gradually and imperceptibly divested of its claims to independent and absolute validity, in the same way as formerly the old clerical asceticism had allowed no independence to the *Humanum*. The *Divinum* was absorbed into the service of a *Humanitas* which was to be ethically independent and aesthetically polished. The final reproach which Luther directed at Erasmus, and at the whole Humanist movement, more or less, was simply: ' Human matters carry more weight with him than divine '.

When Erasmus declared, ' We have brought the world into Christianity ', he was, in fact, speaking for the whole movement. But however hard they worked for a compromise of this kind—and Erasmus and many others were serious and energetic in their efforts—it remained a vain striving. There was always a palpable discrepancy between Humanistic ideals and the Christian conscience. For the latter, in spite of all new developments, was quite unable to leave behind its old, inherent otherworldliness. This dichotomy divided through the middle not only the movement but the individual heart of every Humanist; and this is the reason why the frequent attempts to separate the Humanist movement into a ' Christian ' branch and a ' heathen ' branch have been so unsatisfactory. It started with Petrarch himself, in his *secretus conflictus curarum suarum*; all the wonderful ideals, which he pursued with heart and soul, were damned from the religious point of view as soon as he consulted his beloved Augustine about them. And yet they were too much part of him to be abandoned on that account. He maintained an uneasy acquiescence, accepted the inevitable, and remained dangling between his ideals and an indoctrinated *contemptus mundi*. The significant, final words of his personal confession were: ' Let not my destiny oppose my salvation '.

This was a common experience of the more serious and sensitive Humanists. There is enough renunciation of the world in the works of Coluccio Salutati (d. 1406) to satisfy any mediaeval ascetic. He advocates monkish seclusion and retreat from the ' bottomless pit ' of this world, and then adds ' It is a pit, but I neither can nor wish to escape from it! ' Marsiglio Ficino, lying seriously ill, began to doubt the power of his platonic kind of Christianity to heal either the soul or the body. Pico della Mirandola (d. 1494), who was such a fervent admirer of humanity— ' the happiest and most truly admirable of all living things '— nevertheless preached a fervent sermon to his nephew on the utter vanity of all earthly things. Indeed, just before his death at an early age, when he was under the influence of Savonarola's powerful threats and exhortations, it seemed as though he was on the point of putting the preacher's precepts into practice. Agricola's comments on Petrarch's brother, Gherardo, when he entered the Carthusian order, could equally well apply to the life of a saint: ' Being the elder, and so capable of a better decision (than Petrarch!) he has scorned . . . everything that can seduce our minds with flattery and dangerous temptations . . . '. Erasmus in his younger days wrote an *Epistola de contemptu mundi* almost exactly at the same time as his *Antibarbari*; and in his *Enchiridion* there are some very disparaging words about ' Dame World, a very shady character '.

It would not be difficult to find many more examples. They show that the ' worldly piety ' of the Humanists, which they proclaimed with so much confidence, was not as secure as they would like to claim. The religious threat to their intellectual stability attacked every aspect of their view of life. There was a dark shadow-side to all their passionate love of life and their forced, exaggerated visions of Utopia. Their impressions of the shortcomings of this life were equally exaggerated. Their dreams did not materialize. It must be made clear in any comprehensive account of Humanism that there was a strong element of sheer pessimism in the movement. Modern historical works on the subject have attached too little importance to this. Tearful, melancholy complaints of world-weariness (*acedia*),[1] of *dolendi voluptas quaedam*, intrude everywhere in the works of Petrarch. Our bodies are rotten and decrepit; life is mean, uncertain, transitory, and dissolves into ' dreams and shadows ', ' a puff of air and a thin wisp of smoke '. We aspire to a contempt for death, by way either of stoicism or of semi-Christian precepts, but it is so easy to delude ourselves with this comforting philosophy! For even if our souls are immortal, ' we no longer live as men, once the harmony between body and soul has been destroyed ' (Salutati). And the harmony of body and soul was their greatest ambition! It was quite typical of this aspect of the

---

[1] 'Acedia' was a concept with which monks had long been familiar (meaning boredom with monastic life), but the Humanists gave it a new, worldly sense. The ascetic, other-worldly Middle Ages knew nothing about ' world-weariness '; from their point of view it could not exist.

Humanists that so many of them felt old, weary and worn out at the age of forty, after which they declined into grumpy, soured petulance. Their youthful illusions of ' the joy of living ' (Hutten) had been destroyed by the inevitable experiences of life. Agricola found that his ' spirit was not equal to even the smallest worries ' —and this was the reason why he did not want to get married. But as soon as he was able to live a life of complete freedom, with no responsibilities, in Heidelberg, he was more discontented and unhappy than he had ever been before, and he himself ' knew not the reason for it '.

Then the Humanists looked at the general course of world events. They wrote endlessly about the futility and instability of man's undertakings, about the inevitable, horrible fall awaiting everything great and fine, and about the inconsiderate whims of fortune which were the main cause of it all. Their *humanae miseria conditionis* (Poggio) is a good old mediaeval theme, the theme of Innocent III, but the Humanists had a different view of it in at least one aspect. They no longer approached it exclusively from other-worldly premisses; their interest in actual life revealed to them the true nature of the world. As we have seen, there were some among them who inclined to go back to a renunciation of the world in the Christian ascetic sense, but on the whole they did not seek this refuge without a fight. For the ancients, especially Cicero and Seneca, had shown them the way to stoic resignation, a kind of ' heroic pessimism ' through which all this evil could be personally, subjectively overcome.

And although the whims of fortune can be balanced and counteracted by virtue, Ulrich von Hutten (d. 1523) showed with considerable bitterness and self-irony in his dialogue *Fortuna* how, in spite of everything, all the hopes and efforts of men so often ended in mockery and disappointment. All attempts to influence life were inevitably built on quicksands. The uncertainty of life (see above, p. 141), which was the dominant characteristic of the late Middle Ages, was by no means as strange to the Humanists as appearances might suggest. Even if it were true that the soul died with the body (which they as Christians were not allowed to believe) man would still be as well off after death, they argued, as he was before his birth. ' To feel nothing, to be moved by nothing—who would not rather choose that than fear, disease, pain, worries and troubles? '—as Hutten put it.

In the later stages of Humanism many more features pointed in the same direction. There was the ' fool ', the ' jester ' motif, used most effectively by Erasmus in his *Praise of Folly*. According to him the world is ruled by folly; in fact, folly alone makes life possible.   So the best thing to do is to laugh at mankind—not excepting oneself—to the best of one's ability.   In this book the worldly wisdom of Erasmus, sceptical and full of irony, turns folly to wisdom and wisdom to folly.   There is no trace of a firm belief in human qualities or man's dignity.

Another significant feature of Humanism, which was also an innovation, was the tendency to retreat into a dream-world, to design Utopias.   It shows itself in the form of personal dreams of happiness, such as Erasmus's *Convivium religiosum*, and, perhaps a better example, in Rabelais' *Abbey of Thelème*.   These are plans for a happy life written after the author had quietly abandoned all hope of achieving such happiness in reality.   Other Humanists, on the contrary, planned political and social Utopias—notably, Thomas More and Campanella.   For them, as for Plato, the only way to create an ideal human community would be to subject every aspect of life, even the most intimate personal matters, to a rigid, centralized control and consequent uniformity.   Would it not be true to say that the Humanists thereby unwittingly denied their own belief in the individual and their belief that there was no difference between the virtue of men as individuals and *absoluta et perfecta natura*?

There is no doubt that Italy was not only the birthplace but also the most progressive and flourishing centre of Humanism. When the movement spread into the lands north of the Alps— it came to Germany about the middle of the fifteenth century— it was naturally invested with national forms and characteristics. The most typical feature of German Humanism was that it remained for the most part restricted to scholars and, except in Augsburg and Nuremberg, urban patrician circles had very little to do with it.   The universality and the uninhibited art of living of Italian Humanism were quickly diluted to a stodgy, homely pedantry in Germany.   Schoolroom standards and purposes which were essentially moralistic were brought into the foreground of the movement, obscuring those aesthetic elements of the new Humanism which had distinguished the movement in the south. Among the German Humanists there were very few who really appreciated that the true ideal of southern Humanism was a free, all round, well-balanced personality.[1] Moreover, German Humanism was always more in touch with Christian thought than was Italian Humanism. The religious basis of life was a much more serious concern north of the Alps.

In spite of these limits and weaknesses we can trace quite clearly the characteristics which define the German branch of Humanism.

Rudolf Agricola (d. 1485) combined the usual humanistic studies with considerable artistic talent. He was an active musician and painter; he cultivated his very sensitive temperament assiduously; and he was appreciative of physical beauty and prepared to indulge in sport as an aid to health. Perhaps he came nearer than any other German to the demands of the Italian Humanists for a balanced, harmonious versatility—' a single entity of physical and intellectual endowments ', as Aeneas Sylvius put it.

Willibald Pirckheimer (d. 1530) possessed a library that was unique in Germany, and he fully enjoyed the results of a refined upbringing and humanistic education. As a friend of Dürer he showed himself to be a most understanding and generous patron of art. Either personally or by correspondence he was in touch with all the intellectual leaders of Europe, and he played an essential part in the political life and the wars of Nuremberg, his native town. He enjoyed life like a cultivated man of the world, and, all in all, there was something about him, of that universality typical of the Italian Renaissance. But he was never able to weld all these segmented talents and virtues into a positive creative force.

Conrad Celtis (d. 1508), the German ' arch-Humanist ', as

---

[1] The ideal of the ' universal genius ' (*uomo universale*), particularly when it came to include physical beauty as an essential element, did not emerge before the fifteenth century even in Italy. Perhaps not entirely, but for the most part, it was the result of the middle-class kind of Humanism finding its way into the courts of the princes and there mingling with the old knightly ideals (as in Castiglione's *Courtier*). In Germany there is scarcely a trace of this courtly kind of Humanism.

Friedrich von Bezold called him,[1] was the outstanding German counterpart of those irresponsible and carefree literati so numerous in Italy. He led an unsettled life wandering about Europe from one scientific or literary undertaking to another— and from one love affair to another. He was extremely versatile and so full of plans that he never produced the great works of which he was capable. His life was spent in a twilight of free-thinking scepticism, libertinage and loyalty to the church; he lived as a heathen, but this did not prevent him from being a devoted worshipper of the Virgin Mary, and he died *pie et christianissime*.

Mutian (d. 1526), a canon of Gotha, and the Erfurt group of Humanists with which he was closely connected, represented the most serious threat to the Christian faith in Germany. To Mutian Jupiter, Moses and Jesus Christ, Venus and the Virgin Mary, were almost equally holy. He did, however, insist that such esoteric beliefs (*mysteria*) should be restricted to small groups of initiates, so that ' the beliefs of the masses shall not be weakened thereby '. And after all, Mutian himself wanted to preserve his faith in the old church! Johannes Reuchlin (d. 1522) was a much more positive supporter of the Church, but he still succumbed to the spell of that uncontrolled syncretism that Pico della Mirandola had introduced into Italian Humanism. This consisted in ming-ling Christian belief, Neoplatonic and neo-Pythagorean specu-lation, Jewish cabbala and a number of oriental secret cults, and combining them into a world-religion for all.

The relations of the German Humanists to nature were decided by theories of this kind. For sober, scientific study of the natural sciences—such as, for instance, the work of the mathe-matician and astronomer, Regiomontanus (d. 1476)—was the exception rather than the rule. Natural philosophy and specula-tions about nature were their sole approach to the subject, and what the ancient world had said about such things was revered as dogma for the most part (see above, p. 146). The mystic teachings mentioned above, most of which came from the Orient, led them to fantastic secret theories and practices. Astrology,

---

[1] Fr. von Bezold, ' Konrad Celtis ', *Aus Mittelalter und Renaissance* (Munich, 1918), 82 sqq.

alchemy and sorcery were used in medicine, in psychology (theory of the temperaments), in geology and mineralogy, in their opinion of the basic elements of the world, and in their interpretation of the course of history. Particularly in the form of the horoscope these same influences controlled every detail of daily life. We need only think of Reuchlin, or that universal scholar, Abbot Trithemius (d. 1516), or the adventurer, Agrippa von Nettesheim (d. 1535), in this respect. Even the medicine and philosophy of Paracelsus (d. 1541) were full of such mysticism. Their whole approach to nature was governed by the overpowering theory of the unity and interdependence of the elements of the macrocosm and the human microcosm. Nor was it all pure fantasy; there had always been so many points of contact and so many cross-currents between astrology and astronomy, alchemy and chemistry, sorcery and real methods of controlling nature. But the time for science in the modern sense of the word had not yet come.

Patriotic feeling, which inspired the German Humanists to write their local and national histories, was yet one more aspect that they derived from Italian examples. Celtis, Heinrich Bebel (d. 1518), Beatus Rhenanus (d. 1547), the outstanding pedagogue Jakob Wimpfeling (d. 1528), Cuspinian (d. 1529) and Aventin (d. 1534), were all keen students of the German and Germanic past, right back to the time of Tacitus. Encouraged and rewarded by the Emperor Maximilian, they were enthusiastic, if rather soulful, admirers of the great period of the emperors. The Italians' pride in their own past greatness went hand in hand with their attempts to revive classical literature, but it was not so easy for the German Humanists. How could they praise Arminius as the liberator of Germany and maintain their enthusiasm for ancient Rome, when the Romans were made to appear nothing more than ruthless conquerors? But the Humanists were never very good at adhering to a consistent policy or theory, and the contemporary hatred of clerical Rome (see above, p. 136) provided an easy way out of the dilemma. Nevertheless, the historical efforts of the German Humanists, who were too easily led into the wildest fantasies, were much inferior to the works of the Italians.

Erasmus (d. 1536), the greatest of all the northern Humanists, would have nothing to do with such national distinctions. ' I wish to be a citizen of the world, a friend of all men—or, rather, a stranger to all men '. He was perhaps the first thoroughgoing European; Pope Leo X called him ' the wonder of the west ' and ' bringer of light '. Although he had neither the range of interest nor the sophistication of Agricola or Pirckheimer, he was the most complete representative of the period, having all its strength and all its weaknesses.

Humanism was a product of its age. In common with the period as a whole it represented a retreat from a general, objective outlook to an individual, subjective one. The Humanists went further and aimed at a personal privacy which tended to divorce men from all outside ramifications and encouraged them to regard themselves as individually absolute. This anthropocentric attitude of the Humanists, which was a sublimated, intellectual parallel to contemporary trends in popular religion, brought the divine down to human levels. As they saw it, religion entered into the affairs of men only in so far as it served to confirm their realization of themselves. This self-realization, however, was confined to the ethical and aesthetic plane, and consequently— as in the case of popular religion, only on a more refined level— religion was replaced by morals, and so was gradually deprived of real significance. In this way Humanism failed to establish a solid spiritual foundation; the underlying philosophy and concept of life was never sufficiently integrated or rounded off. The most effective and historically the most fertile achievement of the movement lay in its assertion of personality, of ' belonging to oneself ', and in the vitality with which the Humanists pressed on into new, virgin fields of thought. In these features Humanism was definitely a forerunner of the modern epoch. But it needs only a glance at the movement as a whole to see that it was incomplete and that it could never harvest what it had sown. Because it was incomplete, Humanism never produced any works, either literary or philosophical, which could withstand the passage of what Petrarch called ' the Triumph of Time ', for all the self-conscious effort that was put into writing. What is there of it all that is still worth reading for its own sake? A dozen or so sonnets of Petrarch, with their bewitching soft tones, and a few other poems (but scarcely any by German Humanists); a considerable number of letters, this being, as might be expected, the Humanists' best medium; and Erasmus's *Praise of Folly*.[1]

A monk named Wandalbert wrote in the ninth century: ' It is divine providence that decides for every epoch what is suitable for the human race according to the nature and conditions (*pro modo et ratione*) of the period, so that there is no need for us to yearn for the happiness of our forefathers any more than they need have condemned the conditions of our period, if they had been able to foresee it '. This observation anticipates by a thousand years Ranke's famous sentence: ' Each epoch stands before God alone, and its merits depend not on what develops out of it in history, but on its own existence, its own self '. But there is one essential difference between them: the modern historian, even when he is a pious Christian, in trying to explain the course of history, feels his way cautiously from historical events to their relationship to God, whereas the mediaeval monk was firm in his belief that only a knowledge of God can help us to understand the course of history. Be that as it may, the fact remains that the period of the Middle Ages, in its progress through the centuries, was endowed with exactly what was due to it *pro modo et ratione*. Its values are to be sought in itself. It began with an extremely simple and scanty inheritance, but before it ended it had included all possibilities of human life, thought and feeling —positive and creative as well as negative and destructive—which

[1] There is no authoritative work on the Humanistic movement in Germany, nor on Humanism as a whole; the following are noteworthy works on individual humanists: J. Huizinga, *Erasmus* (New York, 1924); P. S. Allen, *Erasmus* (Oxford, 1934); J. J. Mangan, *Erasmus*, 2 vols. (London, 1940); W. Ruegg, *Cicero und der Humanismus, Formale Untersuchungen über Petrarca und Erasmus* (Zürich, 1946)—important; R. Weiss, *Humanism in England in the Fifteenth Century* (Oxford, 1957); W. F. Schirmer, *Der englische Frühhumanismus* (Leipzig, 1931); J. H. Lupton, *The Life of John Colet* (2nd edn., 1909); R. W. Chambers, *Thomas More* (London, 1935); W. Schrinner, *Castiglione und die englische Renaissance* (Neue deutsche Forschungen, Vol. 234) (Berlin, 1939).—Fr. v. Bezold, ' Konrad Celtis ', *Aus Mittelalter und Renaissance* (Munich, 1918); Fr. v. Bezold, *Rudolf Agricola* (Munich, 1884); C. Burckhardt, ' Willibald Pirckheimer ', *Gestalten und Mächte* (Munich, 1941); E. Zinner, *Leben und Wirken des Johannes Müller von Königsberg (Regiomontanus)* (Munich, 1938); E. Metzke, ' Die " Skepsis " des Agrippa von Nettesheim ', VLit. XIII (1935), 401 sqq.; E. Metzke, ' Mensch, Gestirn und Geschichte bei Paracelsus ', *Blätter für deutsche Philosophie* XV (1941); P. Joachimsen, *Geschichtsauffassung und Geschichtsschreibung in Deutschland unter dem Einfluss des Humanismus*, Part I, (Leipzig, 1910).

the western world could offer both to the individual and to society. Or, at least, it provided the foundations and the early stages of them. By the time that was achieved the Middle Ages had outgrown their original structure; they had reached or already left behind the limits imposed by their own intrinsic nature. The period of the Middle Ages had fulfilled its own law and its own mission and had to give way to a new epoch.

INDEX OF NAMES

STUDIES IN MEDIAEVAL HISTORY

Edited by GEOFFREY BARRACLOUGH

BASIL BLACKWELL . OXFORD